Padayon

A Cebuano Couple's Legacy in Education

BETH SALAZAR VILLARIN

WESTBOW
PRESS®
A DIVISION OF THOMAS NELSON
& ZONDERVAN

WestBow Press books may be ordered through booksellers or by contacting:

WestBow Press
A Division of Thomas Nelson & Zondervan
1663 Liberty Drive
Bloomington, IN 47403
www.westbowpress.com
844-714-3454

All Scriptures are from the ESV® Bible (The Holy Bible, English Standard
Version®), copyright © 2001 by Crossway, a publishing ministry of
Good News Publishers. Used by permission. All rights reserved.

ISBN: 979-8-3850-3896-1 (sc)
ISBN: 979-8-3850-3897-8 (hc)
ISBN: 979-8-3850-3898-5 (e)

Library of Congress Control Number: 2024925040

Print information available on the last page.

WestBow Press rev. date: 02/03/2025

To Daddy and Mommy,

who taught me the virtue ot hard work and
sacrifice, who ventured to new horizons
for the good of the future generations.

Love and kisses,
Abet

"Education is the best investment one can make."

Engr. Doroteo Monte de ramos Salazar
Madridejos, Cebu
April 12, 2017

Contents

Author's Note

There are many areas in my parents' lives which I have no information or no pictures. And that is part of the journey in writing. I tried to capture significant areas of their lives as accurately as I could.

Some names have been changed for privacy reasons. I asked permission from every person whose name, initial, or picture I used, for as long as I had contact with them.

This book uses English, Cebuano, and Tagalog languages (two official languages in the Philippines). There will be English translations whenever Cebuano or Tagalog words will be used. I wanted to capture the original meanings or the words by using the languages used by my parents.

This memoir is meant to recall and cherish the lovely (and not so lovely) experiences daddy and mommy had. Their effort to touch lives has not gone unnoticed.

Prologue

A little over two years ago, on July 23, 2021, during daddy's fourth death anniversary, my siblings were talking about:

"commissioning a writer to make an official biography of Daddy"

"start with an average writer & build on"

"*sayang*' (what a waste) daddy's life if not documented...Daddy's life is a good story...a written page of his life is a good legacy"

"P_____ just asked me where can he read about Papa?"

"MBeth can do it."

"She was telling us (that) she was starting to write something on daddy"

"Best writer would be someone who was close and knew daddy."

"You can do it, MAbet."

I'm trying to find a way to contact *Wikipedia* to add daddy there, under Famous People of Cebu.

"Yes, M. Beth you can do it!"

"Come up with an outline and expectations... Time limits and length of pages, colored or black and white...hard bound or soft bound and Kindle versions. How before a first draft 1-3 yrs or 12-18 month. Budget? Other suggestions? Animated movie?"

I just learned from our Information Technology (IT) department head, that the history in our school site, and that in *Wikipedia*, was actually written by daddy.

That calling was mine, yours truly, Manang Beth, or Manang Abet.

After chatting with almost a hundred family members, friends, past and present employees of my parents, in person or through Facebook Messenger, while looking at lots of pictures, memorabilia, and whatnots, and recalling as much memories about daddy and mommy, I was finally able to put the gazillion bits of information into my very first non-academic publication.

I was able to complete my basic draft in about one hundred days (October to December 2022), as writers are suppose to do. I squeezed whatever time I could, in spite of a full time in-person job and a part-time virtual job. I even wrote (or encoded on my laptop) while waiting for my plane to leave during my travels to Vancouver and Toronto (Canada), and Chiba City (Japan).

Then I had to see my editor on April 30, 2023 during mommy's wake in Cebu. I had to focus on my book and set aside emotional tears. Mommy's passing made me redo the entire *Chapter 3, Where's the Disco*, to include details of her most recent death.

Enjoy reading it as much as I enjoyed writing it!

Acknowledgments

I am giving my ultimate praise and glory to the Lord Jesus almighty who has given me the gift of wisdom and time to create this memoir.

My deep gratitude to my siblings who believe in me.

The same gratitude goes to my elementary and high school teachers of St. Theresa's College, Cebu City, Philippines, who taught me the beauty of the English language through prose and poetry.

Thanks a million to those who have given me a word or a picture, or ten thousand words and pictures, about my parents, some of whom knew daddy and mommy even before I was born.

I have carefully selected details to make this write-up flow smoothly, choosing information and pictures which fit the write-up.

I am likewise thankful for my boss, L.H., for giving me time off to put together this intricate manuscript.

A special thanks to the lovely couple who brought me to my first Book Festival, the *Word Vancouver 2022 Festival* at Simon Fraser University Harbour Centre, Vancouver, Canada, on September 25, 2022. As I saw my friend's husband stand behind the counter, endorsing his book to the passersby, I imagined myself doing the same someday.

A very special thanks to my children and most especially to my husband, Eleno "Jun" Villarin Jr., for giving me time and space to do my book. When I said *"Dili 'ta mangato'g mall karong weekend kay trabahuon nako akong libro."* (We will not go to the mall this weekend since I have to work on my book.) He repeatedly commented, *"Kanus-a pa na mahuman? Inig retire nimo?"* (When will you ever finish? When you retire?)

He understands my passion to write. Thanks again *"Ga!"* Love you!

My gratitude to the SCSIT staff who served as runners for my manuscript to reach my editor, and vice versa, and to those who assisted me with the technicalities of software.

I am fortunate to have a great production team, from my printers to my layout artists. And for Mae Salazar's wonderful improvement of my book cover.

Most of all, I am very pleased with my editor, Marlinda Angbetic-Tan, for her detailed corrections. She even edited my Cebuano words. I have chosen her to edit my book since she had personnally met my parents. She spent time with them in Madridejos during daddy's first term as Mayor.

One

Plan A Didn't Work

"Come to Chong Hua now! Daddy's blood pressure is dropping!"

Cecile sent me a text message, just as I ordered lunch at Shamrock, Fuente. Earlier, Jun and I left quickly right after the mid morning service at the Metropolitan Christian Fellowship, along P. del Rosario Ave., Cebu City.

I hurriedly brought the three orders of our take-out Shamrock's special *pancit* (Filipino noodles) to the suite room of daddy, at the upper floor of the Annex Building of Chong Hua Hospital.

"He's going to die very soon!" was the thought that filled my mind on the way to the hospital. As I walked briskly into daddy's private suite, I saw Cecile, my younger physician sister, holding daddy's pale legs, caressing it gently, as if to alleviate whatever pain he must have been suffering.

It was almost two that Sunday afternoon.

Other family members were in the room but my eyes were glued to daddy, lying still on his hospital bed. He lost a lot of weight since he was first admitted six weeks prior. His dry, disheveled hair was splayed flat on his memory foam pillow. His eyelids were shut tight. His cheek bones emphasized due to thinning muscles and fat. His arms and legs atrophied, close to skin and bones.

His blood pressure was slowly dropping until a straight line appeared on the heart monitor at exactly 3:57 pm. There was a long cold silence. Only the low humming from the central air vent was heard. All eyes stared at the motionless body on the bed, dressed in a hospital gown he hardly wore. The father figure who was once the strongest, toughest man on earth was dead!

Medical personnel slowly trickled in. Some family members filled daddy's room and the adjacent receiving room. As soon as Chris, my nurse son, came, he immediately took out his stethoscope and listened intently for any faint heartbeat which could still be there—searching for any sign of life. He mumbled some sweet inaudible words to daddy, as if saying his silent goodbye to his papa.

Other family members slowly trickled in: the families of Adam, Cecile, Danielle, Eduardo, and Flint, including Tiyo (uncle) Boy—mommy's favorite cousin—and Tiya (auntie) Fannie. Most of the family members were quiet, with a few people sobbing. All eyes were focused on daddy. All were downhearted but I was glad that daddy's suffering was over.

Other hospital staff came in to remove tubes and other attachments from his body. Then they wrapped daddy's pale, cold, rigid body with a plain white cloth, reminding me of Jesus wrapped in strips of linen, in a cave, on that first Good Friday in Jerusalem, 2,000 years ago.

But daddy was NOT God. We, six siblings, however looked up to daddy like a god, but he *was not*. Daddy always portrayed a strong, seemingly invincible persona.

"let his legacy reign and continue to make him proud", on their 58th wedding anniversary. That's me in a blue shirt, wrapping my right arm around mommy's shoulder. The Philippine flag was drapped on daddy's coffin to signify that he was a public servant. (video/photo credit: Emily on Facebook, July 25, 2017)

These are the information written on his death certificate:

3:57 pm, July 23, 2017, In the Certificate of death from the Office of the Civil Registrar General, Republic of the Philippines:

> "81 years old. Immediate cause: Non-Hodgkin's Lymphoma, Antecedent cause: Hospital-acquired Pneumonia, Underlying cause: Hypertensvie Cardiovascular Disease. Doroteo Monte de Ramos Salazar, Male. Occupation: Engineer. Name of Father: Ranulfo Soledad Salazar. Name of Mother: Antonia Mercado Monte de Ramos. Attended by a private physician Dr. Francisco Chio, Jr., Lim M.D., from 07/03/2017 to 07/23/2017."

Hmm, Non-Hodgkin's Lymphoma! I learned that daddy passed away from lymphoma a week or two after his death, when Christine, our loyal office staff, gave me a copy of his official death certificate. I was probably told by one of his doctors of the real cause of his passing, but those words never stuck to my tired, restless brain.

It was just six weeks prior when daddy was checked in a small private room. A week or two later, when his illness was deteriorating, our family decided to move him to a bigger, more expensive suite, allowing space for 36 immediate family members to visit.

Why did anyone not find out about daddy's early symptoms of lymphoma?

As a researcher myself, and a frustrated medical doctor, I intended to find out where we, siblings, or his doctors, missed out (without blaming anyone). I believe that God had predestined daddy to go home, on that fateful 23rd day July 2017, but I wished that he could have stayed longer if only we recognized early symptoms of lymphoma.

I found this abstract which mentioned oral manifestations as areas of early detection of lymphoma, "Oral manifestation of lymphoma: a systematic review", from the National Library of Medicine, August 17, 2016:

> "Lymphoma is a malignant disease with two forms: Hodgkin's lymphoma (HL) and non-Hodgkin's lymphoma (NHL). Non-Hodgkin's lymphoma is diagnosed in extranodal sites in 40% of cases, and the head and neck region is the second most affected, with an incidence of 11-33%, while HL has a very low incidence in extranodal sites (1-4%). The aim of this study was to identify oral manifestations of lymphoma through a systematic literature review.....Among the intraoral findings, the most frequent were ulcerations, pain, swelling, and tooth mobility.....Among the few studies reporting imaging finding, the most cited lesions included hypodense lesions with diffuse bounderies, bone resorptions, and tooth displacements....."

...ulcerations, pain, swelling...tooth mobility issues daddy complained about as early a two years before he passed. Hmmm… early signs of lymphoma? Although Cecile and I knew about his teeth issues all along, we just thought it was the usual dental problem.

When I went home in 2015, I told daddy and mommy that I could not be at the office—which had always been expected of us, siblings, whenever we were visiting Cebu. I was seeing my dentist to have my teeth cleaned.

"Can I see your dentist? I need new *postiso* (Cebuano for dentures)," Daddy immediately asked.

I was happy that daddy was concerned about his dentures and that he was willing to see *my* dentist. This was unusual. Was daddy not content with *his* dentist? I never asked him this question, as I never questioned daddy on any of his decisions. In our Filipino culture, we have so much respect for our elders that we do not dare question them on their decisions, as that would be considered as disrespectful. On the other hand, I was surprised that he was concerned about his teeth, something he had never brought up to me.

"Sige, 'Dy (short for daddy)! It's just across San Carlos. What time?"

"Anytime," he acquiesced.

He got the next available appointment, first thing the following morning. We walked up two flights of stairs to see the dentist. I was relieved to see no line of patients, when there would usually be three to five people waiting. When I opened the door, I was taken aback to see a *different* dentist, not the usual nice and smiling female dentist. It was a male dentist.

"*Nagbakasyon si Dr. J.* (Dr. J. is on vacation)", the secretary explained.

I felt quite uncomfortable, but daddy and mommy were *already* at the clinic. The male dentist looked welcoming anyway. I still wanted daddy to be served by *my* regular dentist, the one who was very open about every procedure she did. I gave short replies as the dental assistant asked me a few questions about daddy's teeth.

"Mr. Salazar?" the male dentist called out.

Daddy stood up and walked to the enclosed dental clinic, with a swinging entrance door and a wooden wall, both of which were not fully flushed to the ceiling. Those in the waiting room would hear every drill sound, each clinking and clanking of dental instruments used. Since I sat close to the swinging door I overheard their conversation. The male dentist sounded professional so I had to trust him.

While waiting, I looked at pictures of men, women and children with picture-perfect white teeth. I was still excited about daddy's decision to see *my* dentist and wondering: Why was he refusing to see his regular dentist? Was he dissatisfied with his service? Did he refuse to accept any information he was told? I did not even know his regular dentist, having spent almost five years abroad. That was Cecile's turf.

I heard daddy complain to the dentist about his teeth issues. The dentist comforted him that *he will take care of it.* After almost an hour sitting on the dental chair, daddy came out telling us that his dentures would be done in a few days. Those new dentures though did not fit him well. He was still in pain after that venture into the dental clinic.

Breakfast time at home. May 2017.

In my next trip home the following year, I saw that daddy lost weight. He looked different, not the healthy-looking daddy that I always remembered. I noticed that he ate less and chose soft food—usually *lugaw* (rice porridge) or *sabaw* (soup)— causing him to have sunken cheeks, a smaller face, and less body mass. He said that this teeth hurt when he ate hard food.

His teeth issues must have been on-going. Hmm? That kept me wondering again. Was daddy really getting so sick? I refused to believe it.

Cecile always managed to schedule daddy and mommy for their medical and dental yearly check-up. Nothing abnormal with their health, just the usual health concerns they were dealing with. Those frequent doctor's visits to Dr. Chio, Cecile's friend, made him like family to us. Dr. Chio and his wife invited us over for special meals in their lovely home during family celebrations. The couple brought lots of food to daddy's Chong Hua suite during his last days. Daddy and mommy were not really close friends with their dentist, but I had hoped that their doctor and dentist shared notes.

In the spring of 2017, our family made plans for daddy and mommy to visit Anthony (my eldest son) and Sayo, his Japanese wife, and their two kids in Chiba City, Japan. That could have been the perfect moment for them to see their first great grandson, Daiki. They had met their first great granddaughter, Aika, a few years back during a Cebu visit. Daddy's health issues hindered them. On top of that, a family member, who was supposed to accompany both of them, was not able to complete his travel documents.

The Japan trip was cancelled.

Then there was another plan for daddy and mommy to visit Eduardo, my younger brother in Australia, and at the same time watch the Manny Pacquiao—the Greatest Filipino boxer— boxing match! It was going to be exciting! Eduardo had bought the boxing tickets—much higher than the regular price. This was also cancelled!

Travel arrangements were made. A few weeks before the departure date, daddy complained of a sharp, intense pain on his leg, saying that it was too painful for him to walk. He was brought to see his doctor who recommended physical therapy. He went to the first few P.T. sessions, but the pain did not go away. It was just a symptom of a deeper, more serious, more complicated issue… something abnormally present in his body.

Mommy and their helpers quickly packed daddy's belongings. He had to be confined in Chong Hua for a series of medical exams. Although he was *reluctant to go*, he had no choice.

I was monitoring daddy's predicament, through Facebook messages with my siblings, while working through three part-time jobs—an early childhood education, a personal support worker, a private caregiver for kids or the elderly—in Ottawa, Ontario, Canada. I was, at the same time, taking care of my family. It was barely two months since my last visit when Daddy's pain was sudden and totally unexpected. I read about daddy's deterioration word for word, day and night for many weeks on end, in our family chat group..... until one afternoon, I couldn't bear it anymore.

Shortly after noon, on June 14, 2017, Wednesday, while I was getting ready for my afternoon shift at Jackson Trails Early Learning Centre in Stittsville, I got word that daddy *needed* a cane to walk from his hospital bed to the washroom!

Daddy needing a *cane*?! I'm going home!...was my first instinctive thought.

I wanted to board the first available flight home. But I had to inform my employers, my school, and my family about this emergency. It would only take a day at least to do that, I thought.

I never expected that daddy would ever need help with mobility. Although he turned eighty-one on his last birthday, he always bragged that he could still climb stairs. But this time, he could hardly get off the bed by himself. Something was terribly wrong. Daddy's mobility issues were difficult to accept. A week after he was confined, not only was it difficult for him to get out of his hospital bed, *it was also difficult for him to go to the washroom with a cane, by himself.* His legs lost the strength to carry his body. His grandsons took turns assisting him with a seemingly simple job that my eighty-two-year-old mom could not possibly do by herself.

Early the next morning, I emailed the Registrar's office at Algonquin College, telling them that I had to drop the two online summer classes for the Early Childhood Education diploma course I was registered in. I was halfway through the course. Now I had to put it on hold. Although my second career was important to me, my dad's health was my priority.

At around 5 pm on June 15, 2017, Thursday, I bought plane tickets for Jun, my husband, Xirus, my youngest son, and myself for Cebu City, Philippines, even if it would cost about 23% more than the regular plane fare.

As I grabbed my summer outfits from our bedroom closet in our Kanata condo, a lot of BIG questions raced through my mind:

Is daddy going to die?

Who is going to take care of mommy when most of us are abroad? Who is going to manage our multi-million businesses?

And little questions:

How long will Jun, Xirus, and I stay in Cebu?

Will all of my siblings and their kids come in time to see daddy, while he still breathes?

When will be our—Jun, Xirus, and myself—first overnight duty, as daddy's personal caregivers?

Air Canada Flight number 287 bound for Toronto is now ready for boarding at Gate 23. We are boarding passengers on Zone 1. Please ensure that you have your ID, passport and boarding passes ready for verification.

We boarded the plane five hours after I bought our tickets. It was ten in the evening. Jun, Xirus, and I lined up in front of Gate 23, at the Macdonald–Cartier International Airport, in Ottawa, bound for Seoul, with a two-hour layover in Toronto. From Seoul, Korea, we went to Cebu. It was the longest trip I ever took.

While the plane was taking off, I thought about the worse that could happen to daddy. He was always the strong man in our family, rarely getting sick, seldom complaining of any kind of pain, never been in the hospital, as far as I recalled. He and mommy had a healthy diet of soup—a staple for every meal—with rice, fish, chicken, veggies, and fruit. Occasionally they had a cup of ice cream for dessert. They were both non-smokers nor were they wine, beer, or *tuba* (coconut wine) drinkers. In fact, daddy claimed that *he was allergic to alcohol.*

When daddy or mommy got really sick, they did not tell us. Invariably, they would fly to Manila, as they frequently did for business, to get medical help there. I just recently learned about their medical-escapade from a close family member.

The flight almost took thirty hours. Since Cebu is 12 hours ahead of Ottawa, we missed a day. We arrived close to midnight on Saturday, June 17. Roy, the family driver, picked us up at the airport and whisked us straight to Chong Hua. With luggage in our hands, and with heavy hearts, we slipped into daddy's private suite.

"Daddy! Abét here!" I immediately rushed to his bedside.

Daddy always called me "Abét" since birth.

I took his left hand—cherishing every nanosecond of its warmth and tenderness—before I placed it lightly on my forehead (making "amen": a Filipino custom for respecting the elders) then laid it down gently on his bed. A deep silence filled the room.

Daddy did not smile, just breathing silently, as he stared lovingly at me his eldest daughter. His pale face revealed deep hidden pain, the only outward manifestations of weakness were on his extremities, and a discomfort no one understood.

"What happened, 'Dy?" I asked affectionately.

"I'm *yayay*," Daddy answered softly . "*Yayay*" is our family term for feeling sick or getting hurt.

No other words were said.

Why couldn't his treasures, being one of the richest former Mayors of the province, heal him? I was extremely baffled.

Our first night in Chong Hua was our first overnight duty for daddy. Mommy slept in a couch, on the right side of daddy, while I slept in a couch on his left side. We barely caught up with our sleep, after travelling for over a day the night before. But we were eagerly willing to relieve his grandsons, who hadn't had a good night's sleep for several nights in a row.

"Nghh! nghhh! Nghhhhhhh!" Daddy moaned at 2:23 am.

I was startled! At first I thought that it was just a dream. But then the moaning got louder, and louder...and louder. And it didn't stop! Then I realized it was *not* a dream.

He was sitting halfway on his bed, having pushed both of his hands against his bed to support himself up. He stared sideways at me. Daddy needed *my* help. Since he did not say anything else I figured he needed help to the bathroom. He had no strength even to call "Abét!". Jun and Xirus were both in deep slumber. They could not help.

I had no time to think. I had no time for tears. I *had* to help him since no one else could. I wanted him to get better... soon....very soon. I could not afford to see him so, so sick. It was unbearable.

I jumped out of the couch. Half-awake, I went around daddy's right side of the bed, helped him lift both legs from the hospital bed, bent down to tuck his soft bedroom slippers on, and grabbed his walker—replacing the cane a few days earlier—then placed the handle in front of him. I helped him walk slowly to the bathroom—placing my left hand behind his back, in case he may fall over backwards.

Only then did I understand why it took half an hour for one of my elderly clients to reach the bathroom with her walker. Only then did I realize that daddy's strength was incredibly failing.

The half hour ordeal seemed like forever! It was certainly a double ordeal for daddy. He used all his capability to heed nature's call.

Daddy spoke very little during his last weeks in the hospital. He used a lot of his strength for each whisper. Each day in Chong Hua did not seem to make any difference. I saw frustration and helplessness on his face. One day, daddy looked at me with a frown, while pressing his left leg.

"*Hilot* (massage in Cebuano) 'Dy?", I asked him as he nodded. As I gently massaged his thighs and legs, he closed his eyes in temporary relief from the pain he must have felt.

On our third overnight shift, a week later, daddy's health had severely deteriorated. He no longer had any strength even to sit up on his bed. He could barely keep his back straight. Subsequently, he became incontinent. *Whew!* No more bathrooms walks—a momentarily relief for the caregivers.

Several doctors visited daddy to inform us about potential life-threatening complications. Unable to fully comprehend medical terms, we trusted Cecile to decide. After a series of informal sibling discussions, we opted for NO, to operations. At 81, daddy's best option was a maintained comfortable quality of life.

We gave him everything he wanted—his favorite NBA basketball games 24/7 and his favorite food, although this time it had to be pureed. While watching his ballgames on the big television screen, placed high enough on the wall in front of him, he had *Sunburst* chicken, *Casino Español lengua* (ox tongue), even *Snow Sheen pancit guisado* (sauteed noodles). He loved his mealtimes. A week later daddy could barely swallow even pureed food. We used gauze wrapped in a large popsicle stick—Cecile's invention—to lick his meals.

"I'm taking my coffee break!" I told daddy as I was getting sleepy one afternoon.

"Give me coffee." Daddy managed to whisper.

"Sige 'Dy", I smiled at him. He closed his eyes in anticipation of his favorite drink.

I made him *Nescafe* with sugar, dipped gauze in it, and lifted the gauze into daddy's mouth. I felt that my role as caregiver was vital to his existence, as his caring presence was essential to me as an infant— our roles were now reversed.

As a CEO of a self-made conglomerate, daddy wrote as much as his strength would allow. Eduardo sat back-to-back with daddy so that he could write his turn-over procedures for his family. He scribbled notes in a notebook Adam gave him, guiding us what to do. Without any apparent written Succession Plan in place, he *had* to do this by then. He *had* to turn over his earthly possession, duties, and responsibilities, before he would see the last light of day. Someone had to run the school, someone had to look after his real estate and construction businesses, someone had to run the Rural Bank of Madridejos, someone had to implement his other unfinished businesses. He was running out of time. His voice and hands were failing...but his mind was not. Whatever he could *not* write, he *told* Adam what to do. Whenever Adam asked him questions about what he wrote, he answered quickly in a whisper. He *had* an answer for everything. He —with mommy's great help—was a self-made millionaire.

Writing a Succession Plan on his death bed was farthest in our minds, as it was from his. My siblings and I were teary-eyed as we watched him scribble notes. He had lots of things in his mind yet he could only write so much. His very light handwriting strokes revealed his weakness. His one-man show was dimming. Plan B for his six children: Adam, Beth, Cecile, Danielle, Eduardo and Flint, was inevitable.

How could it end so soon, while most of us were at the peak of our careers in foreign lands? How could anyone of us manage their ongoing projects when we only knew fragments about them? Why did I not heed their advice to help the school years ago when I could have worked side-by-side with them? Was it *really greener on the other side of the fence?* Regretful thoughts started to fill my mind.

While it took them a lifetime to build their businesses, would those impromptu scribbled notes be enough to guide us? Although mommy was still with us, it was daddy who mapped it all out. He was the General Builder of our family treasures, the brain of the clan. He got it all mapped out way before we were born.

Plan B for his political career was also being handed over. Romeo Villaceran was the last name on daddy's Nokia cell phone. Daddy sent two messages to Romeo. The first one: "SULOD BALIK OG POLITIKA", ("go back to politics", in Cebuano), in all caps. The second message was blank.

Politics was the last thing they talked about. Romeo ran for Mayor of Madridejos in 2016, the year before daddy passed, but he lost. In the early part of 2017, daddy texted Romeo "to (run for public office) *so that you can help the poor people of Madridejos.*"

As daddy's and mommy's former working student (including mixing coffee for them every morning) in the eighties, Romeo was diligent. Daddy paid for his college education after which he became a licensed Civil

Engineer. He was promoted to Project Engineer for many of daddy's multi-million projects. While daddy was active in politics, his construction business slowed down, thus releasing Romeo from their firm.

On his own, Romeo was able to build his construction firm, with daddy's help. Knowing that Romeo had what it took to run for public office, daddy requested him to run *again* for public office. As a former Mayor of Madridejos, daddy had a passion for public service. He knew that a trustworthy public servant could move mountains, in the person of Romeo who was a native of the town.

On the third week of his hospital stay, as I was about to buy some snacks across Chong Hua Hospital, I bumped into Omê—mommy's distant cousin and Head of the SCSIT Madridejos campus—by the elevator lobby. He and his sons paid daddy a visit after Dr. Serapion Sotto, SCSIT Cebu main campus Director and one of the original school employees, informed him about daddy's grave illness. I was shocked to see them. *Who leaked the secret?* We agreed among our siblings not to inform the public that dad was really sick. It was *bad publicity*, we thought.

Musta daddy nimo? (How is your daddy?)

Ok ra siya. (He is ok.)

Without any elaboration, I gave the simplest answer without revealing anything else. He and his wife worked at the Madridejos school campus, as liaisons of my parents. They had the right to know about daddy's situation but I just could not tell them. It was a deep secret which we wanted to keep, for a very long time. As soon as I talked to them I ended the conversation quickly. Their faces looked so worried, as much as mine.

How could anyone dare tell him? Were they in Chong Hua to verify rumours of his illness? What if they knew that daddy was very ill? What if our employees, students and other clients knew about it? The worstcase scenario could have been chaos, total chaos! The school could have been in disarray if they had known the truth.

Dr. Sotto must have had a feeling that daddy was ill. Well, why couldn't he not fail to notice? Adam was suddenly meeting the school staff during the past weeks. He never did that before. Daddy always presided in all school meetings. Two of our caregiver graduates were even hired to take care of daddy on twelve-hour shifts, for about three days, until they left for other high-paying jobs. Arlyn, the school Assistant Cashier and working student, was also assigned to be one of daddy's caregivers for awhile. These out-of-the-ordinary changes signalled some kind of urgency, very unusual yet obvious, that daddy *was very sick.* Still, we thought we could keep the secret.

But we had far too many things to worry about. We were too overwhelmed, too exhausted, and too confused about everything that was unfolding. We had no time to think, no time to breathe, no time to let the world know that we were in a quandary.

Proverbs 16:9

English Standard Version (ESV)

The heart of man plans his way, but the LORD establishes his steps.

Two

King of Engineers

"By the authority vested in me, by the Board of Directors of Cebu Institute of Technology, for having earned the highest grade among all the engineering graduates of Batch 1957, I now proclaim you, Doroteo Monte de Ramos Salazar, King of Engineers of Batch '57!"

This was *probably* proclaimed by CIT's Registrar at the height of the Graduation Rites in March 1957. Four years before I was born, daddy was King of Engineers! The mathematician of the whole engineering batch. He could give the square root of any 3-digit number in under 2 seconds!

How amazing is that!!!. He wasn't just King of Engineers but he was also Summa Cum Laude, graduating Civil Engineering at the age of 21.

Daddy's graduation picture with his mom and siblings. (L-R standing) Tiyo Boy, Auntie Flor, Tiyo Nito, daddy. (L-R front) Tiyo Billy, Lola Tonyay, his mom, Tiyo Ludy. 1957. (photo credit: Auntie Flor)

As I was growing up, I saw the King of Engineers picture hung on a wall of his basement office in our home. It did not mean much to me until I needed help with my high school Algebra. I was an A-B student, but in Mathematics and Algebra, I was a B-.

One late week night, I knocked at the door of my parents' room.

"Daddy, help me with my homework".

After daddy cracked open the door, I handed him my Algebra notebook showing my handwritten homework which I carefully copied from Miss Abellon's blackboard. *Please* and *Thank you* were non-existent in our English-speaking household.

He wrote answers on my notebook as quickly as he could, without saying a thing. After five minutes, he gave it back to me. Without saying

Good Night—which is also non-existent in our household—I grabbed my notebook, thrilled that I *had* answers in my notebook.

When I reached my room, I stared at the answers. They did *not* look familiar. The manner in which daddy solved the problems were quite different from the way Miss Abellon taught us. Nevertheless I *had* answers to my homework, and that was all that was needed. I did not bother analyzing daddy's answers as long as I had them. It was all that mattered.

My next problem was studying for the Algebra exam. I did not want to ask daddy anymore since it would be difficult for a fifteen -year-old to understand his engineering-level explanation. I wanted a step-by-step solution, showing how all the variables were transformed into a single answer. Mathematical wizards skip lines—solving them mentally— going straight to the solution.

Daddy, the mathematical wizard. 1957.

Talking about Mathematical wizards, daddy must really have been one! He beat a certain wizard who claimed to be the *Greatest Mathematician of the World* during daddy's college days! There was a competition to solve an extremely complex mathematical equation which none of the CIT instructors or this *Greatest Mathematician* could solve. Daddy was the only one who solved it! (using his own way of analyzing and solving)

Daddy is sitting on a wicker chair beside his mom, Lola Tonyay. His siblings are around him. Fiive younger siblings were not born yet. He is between 3-4 years old. His prominent forehead and sharp-looking eyes are quite distinct. 1939-1940, Gakat, Southern Leyte. (photo credit: Auntie Flor)

I struggled with Algebra all throughout high school and college. I had to memorize the pattern of the solution. If there was no pattern, I got lost. It was difficult for me to solve them mentally. Daddy could. He had an abstract mind. I had a visual mind. I had to see everything in writing. Numbers were his game. Letters were mine.

His excellence in numbers *made* him who he was. His compassion for others was another trait. He had the heart to help the poorest of the poor, the underprivileged, the minorities, the outcast of society.

Daddy was always willing to help, even if he dipped into his hard-earned money, to give others the chance. Although daddy's father, Lolo (grandfather) Nene and his mother, Lola (grandmother) Tonyay, were well educated in the best universities in Manila in the late 20s, their meager incomes had to be shared with daddy's nine other siblings.

Daddy was born on February 4, 1935, in Maasin, Southern Leyte, as Doroteo Monte de ramos Salazar, with *Dodô* or *Dô* as his nicknames. As a Rural Municipal doctor, Lolo Nene did not earn much. Despite that, he refused payment from really impoverished patients. He was passionate about healing the sick. Daddy's compassion for the poor was influenced by his dad.

To make ends meet, Lola Tonyay taught Home Economics at St.Thomas Aquinas College in Sogod, Southern Leyte. During one of my Saturday visits to my grandparents' place in Riverside, Labangon, lola once told me that she got 100 in Home Economics. No wonder all her windows had crocheted curtains, with elaborate designs. She also gave my sisters and me a tatted veil each.

While their ten children were growing up in Gakat, they sheltered their family in a large native home, with bamboo flooring and a *nipa* (palm) thatched roof. Lolo's clinic, at the basement of their home, was most convenient for raising their children.

Salazar family and pet dog. Sogod, Southern Leyte. Early 50s. (photo credit: Auntie Flor)

With Lolo being very strict and conservative, he scolded his patients (including family members) when they did not take care of themselves and got very sick. *Letche, letche, letche!* was his favorite curse word. Yet he eventually treated them, anyway. His scolding was probably a *gentle reminder* that had they sought help when the illness was at its onset, it wouldn't have gotten to be that bad.

While the whole world lived through the covid pandemic, washing hands before and after meals was necessary to combat the Coronavirus. That was Lolo Nene's requirement in the Salazar household long before pre-covid times.

Inspite of good personal hygiene, Lolo Nene contracted tuberculosis in the 50s. In the absence of modern medicines, Lolo got so sick that he had to stop his practice to recuperate. He lost one lung after a long treatment. He went back to his practice but on a very limited capacity. Incidentally this was the time when daddy and his siblings were going to college.

As fourth in the brood of ten, daddy felt obliged to augment their parents' income. His three oldest siblings had either gone to Manila or Cebu for their college education. They also sent other money home, but it was not enough. Earning money was not new to daddy. As a young lad, he used to sell peanuts and ice drop (native popsicle). At the end of a hard day's work, he shared his income with his siblings for their daily allowance or for their school needs. That was very heartwarming!

He was able to manage his time so well that he graduated *Salutatorian* from Gakat Elementary School, in Libagon, and *Valedictorian* from St. Thomas Aquinas College, in Sogod.

Going to the same high school with his siblings was fun! Not only did he excel academically, he also excelled in sports! He was the Captain-ball (team captain)—and point guard—of his all-Salazar-brothers (Nito, Boy, Billy, Bebing) basketball team. They used to *terrorize* every other team in the town, winning game after game.

SEVEN HUNTERS
M - Joe Palanca - Manager   C - Dody Salazar - Captain

Daddy (number 8 handwritten on his chest) was 16 then, Captain of the 'Seven Hunters' local basketball team of Sogod, Southern Leyte. Tiyo Billy, (number 9), his younger brother, was part of the team. 1952.

In 1952, when daddy was at the tender age of 16, he was already speculating what to take up in college. He was informed that his dad's younger brother, Engr. Aurelio *Dodóng* Soledad Salazar was the Head of the Surveying Department at Cebu Institute of Technology, as well as an instructor at the same institution. Daddy wanted to go to Cebu City (the neighboring big island) to pursue his education but he needed an affordable place to stay. His parents could not afford a dormitory or apartment for him. It was beyond their budget.

"Tiyo Dodóng gusto unta ko moeskwela sa CIT. Pwede ko mahimog assistant nimo sa Surveying Department?" (Uncle Dodóng, I want to go to school in CIT. May I be your assistant at the Surveying Department?)

Daddy would have spoken those words to Lolo Dodóng in his native dialect, a variation of the Cebuano dialect.

"Unya mentras mahimo ko og assistant nimo, pwede sad ko mopuyo sa inyong lugar ni Tiya Nena?" (Then, while I would be your assistant, may I stay with you at your home with Auntie Nena?)

"Mao ba? Unya unsa diay imong kuha-on?" (Really? So what are you going to take up?)

"Mag abogado unta ko pero murag dili ko angay. Mag engineer nalang ko." (I wanted to be a lawyer but I don't think it fits me. I want to be an engineer instead.)

"Hinuon, bright man sad kag math, bagay gyud ka mag engineer." (Well, you are bright in math anyway, being an engineer would fit you.)

Lolo Dodóng had enough hard-earned wealth but the couple had no children to share their wealth with. Through their kindheartedness, they were able to provide for the schooling of several youth, including daddy.

As soon as his parents and uncle agreed to this arrangement and all preparations were made, daddy boarded the next boat and headed for prosperous Cebu City, the Queen City of the South. Lolo Dodóng provided daddy and his cousins (Noni, Jean, and Dodo Bañez) a room under the stairs of the his two-storey home, along Sanciangco Street, in the heart of the city. Daddy was officially Lolo Dodóng's *working student.* In return for free rent and a small allowance, daddy had to scrub floors and wash dishes.

Now that he had a place to stay, the next problem was getting a scholarship from CIT. His first few months at CIT was not easy. Although he graduated valedictorian in high school, he was top of only about twenty students. A strong typhoon during daddy's senior high school year prevented several of his classmates to finish high school.

His valedictorian award could have been the basis for daddy to be accepted as an academic scholar but the school's Registrar was not convinced of his honor status. The Registrar initially denied him the scholarship but since daddy was very persistent, the Registrar elevated the request to Dr. Nicolas G. Escario, CIT's Founder and first President. The confident young man expressed his request before the President. Surprisingly, he was granted admission, on one condition: *That he be placed in the top section, among the valedictorians of Cebu City and the neighboring schools of the province, and that he top that class during the Mid Term exam!*

What a tall order! But he was *in* for the challenge.

Another problem came up: he had to find ways to pay his school fees and augment his living allowance—until he got the scholarship. Although he was receiving minimal allowance from Lolo Nene and Lolo Dodóng, it was still not enough to cover the city's expensive college lifestyle. Since Lolo Dodóng was Head of the Surveying Department, daddy requested Lolo Dodóng to take him in as a working student at the Surveying Department. Pulling strings together, he got the job!

On top of that, daddy shined boots at the *Plaza Independencia* (a tourist site) on weekends. During those days shiny black, brown or white leather or leatherette shoes or boots were a fad. No wonder daddy had a complete set of shoe-shining kit, complete with black or brown *biton* (shoe shining wax), which he used to shine his leather shoes before he went to the office daily. He sat at the top of the stairs leading to their bedroom, got a cut-out piece of an old white t-shirt, wrapped it around his index and middle fingers, used a wooden shoe brush to buff his shoes of dirt, and rub shoe polish on it (careful to match its color). After letting them dry for a few minutes, he used another piece of a clean cut-out t-shirt, held both ends while placing the middle part of the cloth on the shoe, then buffed the shoes with several quick right-to-left (and vice versa) strokes until it shone all over.

Having juggled work and school earlier in life, he was able to manage his allowances to pay for his school and his living expenses. After he topped the Mid-term exams, he was granted a full academic scholarship!

His full scholarship meant a lot to him.

He was able to prove to his classmates and the school president that intelligence is not determined by the number of students of the graduating class and the status of the school where one comes from. It is a product of personal effort and diligence. He may have come from a high school of less graduates but his intelligence proved that he was able to compete with the topnotch graduates of Cebu!

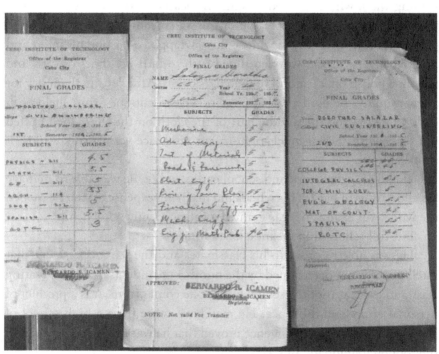

Earning the highest grade possible in most of his First and Second year subjects, 1954-1956.

HONOR R...

COLLEGE OF COMMERCE
First Semester—1953-1954
FIRST YEAR
1. Sable, Bernardo —5.68
2. Tau, Liberato —5.00
3. Fadul-on, Alberto —4.75
4. Enriquez, Rodulfo —4.58
5. Jamili, Jose —4.10
SECOND YEAR
1. Pelicano, Arsenio —4.90
2. Layese, Josefina —4.87
3. Barrera, Gaudencio —4.60
4. Adlawan, Eleazar —4.40
5. Tidoso, Antonio —4.30 M
THIRD YEAR
1. Bradbury, Lydia —4.60
2. Daruca, Marcelino —4.60
3. Mercado, Alejandro Jr. —4.30
4. Baclayon, Daniel —4.20

COLLEGE OF ENGINEERING &
ARCHITECTURE
First Semester—1953-1954
ENGINEERING—I
1. Salazar, Doroteo —ME—5.10
2. Abellanoza, Pilar —CE—5.02
3. Obenza, Arsenio —ME—4.79
4. Escobarte, Arcangel —CE—4.70
5. Paca, Luz —Che—4.57
6. Kintanar, Alfonso Jr. —ME—4.50
7. Alfafara, Achilles —EE—4.41
8. Escario, Celestino —ME—4.19
9. Cuizon, Carlos —ME—4.07
10. Batayola, Cipriano —ME—4.00
11. Aguilar, Roberto —ME—4.29 M
12. Balderas, Julian —ME—4.21 M
13. Juntilla, Roberto —EE—4.19 M
14. Descallar, Letecio —CE—4.14 M
CE—II
1. Alvarez, Telesforo —4.41
   Gaviola, Gaudioso —4.41
2. Flores, Wilfredo —4.25
3. Galope, Samuel —4.07
4. Aleman, Fortunato —4.11 M
ME—II
1. Fuentes, Siegfredo —5.00

2. Galindo, Florello —4.88
3. Gemina, Editho —4.30
4. Osorio, Eugerly —4.93 M
EE—II
1. Biton, Jaime —4.68
2. Tagalog, Juanito —4.30
3. Kintanar, Miguel —4.12
CE—III
1. Caseñas, Elpidio —4.65
2. Silvela, Ernesto —4.15
3. Laput, Ireneo —4.13 M
ME—III
1. Despe, Oscar —5.08
2. Polancos, Cristobal —5.02
3. Bagulo, David —4.38
EE—III
1. Tan, Siao Set —5.00
2. Mantilla, Ledoven —4.45
3. Paredes, Reynaldo —4.05 M
CE——IV
1. Montesa, Guido —4.48
2. Simon, Bienvenido —4.29
ME—IV
1. Buendia, Honorato —4.18
EE—IV
1. Emata, Gilbert —4.10
ARCH. I
1. Creus, Antonio —4.48
ARCH. III
1. Diaz, Plutarco —4.00 M
ARCH. IV
1. Tan, Ricardo —4.88

Highest Average in Eng'g. & Arch.
Dorotheo, Salazar, ME—5.10

NOTE: M — means with Merits—
having one 3 or two 3.5's. All others
with honors.

TEACHERS COLLEGE
First Semester—1953-1954
EDUCATION
1st Year
1. Abella, Celestina —4.03 M
2. Babol, Felicidad —4.02 M
(Continued on page 27)

The TECHNICIAN

"Highest Average in Eng'g & Arch. Dorotheo, Salazar, ME-5.10": The TECHNICIAN, school publication of Cebu Institute of Technology, 1954.

Cebu City is a first class highly-urbanized city in the Central Visayas region of the Philippines and the capital of Cebu Province. According to the 2020 census, it had a population of 964,169 people, making it the sixth most populated city in the nation, and the most populous in the Visayas. Sogod, Southern Leyte, on the other hand, is a second class municipality, with a population of 47,552 in 2020, with barely 5% of Cebu City's population.

During daddy's college days in the 50s, Sogod's population could have been 15-20% as of that of Cebu City's population. An average *probisyano* (country lad) would be *very timid* to excel in the big city of Cebu. Daddy broke that stereotype. He was *not* the average *probisyano*. He was an achiever! He was smart, intelligent, very ambitious, and full of guts—a risk-taker!

Seeing daddy's prowess in mathematics, Lolo Dodóng gave him a teaching load while he was still a sophomore. He started teaching Surveying and other engineering subjects to freshmen. Eventually, he was given teaching loads to teach higher level students.

Daddy was a great negotiator. When he was a freshman working student in the Surveying Department, one of his jobs was Property Custodian of the surveying instruments. He had no problem with that. His only problem was when the students returned the instruments so late at night, having come from far-flung surveying sites.

Commuting late at night in those days was very inconvenient. Instead of paying fare for a *jeepney* (minibus-like public utility vehicles very popular in the Philippines) or a *tartanilla* (two-wheeled carriage drawn by a single horse, popular in the 40s and 50s), daddy bought a used bike. Biking home on late nights, along dimly-lit streets, was not only unsafe and but it was also too tiring for daddy.

Pa-ita ani oi! Libre lagi kug kapuy-an pero maglampaso ug maghugas pakog plato! Wala na koy oras magtu-on ani! Unsa-on nalang! (This is terrible! I may have free rent but I still have to scrub floors and wash dishes! I do not have time to study anymore! What can I do about this?) Daddy must have thought to himself.

He found another way out!

Pwede ko matug sa eskwelahan sa semana nga ting klase kay kadaghanan gabii na kaayo iuli ang mga surveying instruments sa mga estudyante. (I may sleep in school during weekdays when there are classes since the students usually return their surveying instruments so late at night.) Lolo Dodóng was aware of the returning habits of the students and so he granted daddy's request.

"When I was in college, I had the biggest house! I slept in CIT as a working student. I slept on a Chemistry lab table and used the Bunsen burner to cook my food!" Daddy would brag to his children and grandchildren over mealtimes. Although daddy had an iron-top table to sleep on, he padded it with a flattened carton box.

The Chemistry building. It is here where many a wonderment were opened to us.

His bedroom while he was a working student in CIT. 1950s.

The Library building.

His other bedroom.

Daddy's (second row, 5th from the right) class with Lolo Dodong (second row, 6th from the right). Cebu Institute of Technology. Mid 50s.

"*Sa una ang iya(ng) pillow(s) books ang (iyang) mat carton mama's love baby oil/powder!*" (before his pillows were books and his mat was a carton of Mama's Love Baby Oil/Powder). Danny, a former working student, narrated to me what daddy told him.

Daddy had two choices to sleep in: Lolo Dodóng's storeroom, located under the stairs of the Library, or the Chemistry lab. Part of daddy's duties was to clean the storeroom containing his uncle's edited surveying books. He kept his personal belongings in carton boxes under the Chemistry tables. When students or teachers asked him what was inside those boxes, he simply said that they contained lab apparatus.

Doing laundry was interesting.

Nia ang akong bulingon aron malabhan ni mamá. (Here are my dirty clothes for my mom to wash.) Every weekend, he requested a boat crew member of the shipping line plying the weekly Maasin-Cebu route, to deliver his dirty laundry (in boxes) to his mom, Lola Tonyay, in Sogod, the neighboring town to Maasin. It took 10 hours for the box to reach her. As soon as the clothes were dry, they were shipped back to daddy through the same route.

Even as a first grader, daddy knew his capabilities. Tiya Jean, daddy's first cousin, told me this story. When daddy and Tiya Inday, Tiya Jean's older sister, were classmates in grade one, the Second World War broke out from 1941 to 1946. As soon as classes resumed, students of different ages attended the same class on the first day of school.

"Kinsay naka sogod ug grade one adtong wala pay gira? (Who of you started grade one before the war broke out?), " a teacher asked.

"Ako! (I), "my ten-year-old daddy replied, as he raised his hand confidently and eagerly.

Daddy was promoted to second grade, while Tiya Inday remained in first grade. He was always promoted to the next grade until he was supposed to be promoted to the class of Tiyo Boy, his older brother.

"Genius siguro to siya kay sigi man siya gipromote!, (He must have been a genius since he was always promoted!)" Tiyo Mat (daddy's younger brother twelve years his junior) observed.

Lolo Nene was furious!!! He barged into the principal's office of Tiyo Boy's elementary school.

"Leche! Leche! Leche! Ayaw na ipromote si Dodo kay ma da-ut si Boy ug pareho silag grado! (Stop promoting Dodo since Boy will be affected if they will be in the same grade!)."

There was a time when his overconfidence for mathematics cost him his pride. This time it was for the Civil Engineering board exam. Adam related to me that since he was *super confident that he mastered the mathematics subject,* he did not review for that subject for the board exam. He was short of a *simple and basic math question*, which made him only second best, 2nd Placer in the C. E. board exams. Frustrated with himself, he reviewed *all* the subjects (including mathematics) for the Geodetic boards. He got 1st Place this time!

Nothing stopped him from learning something new. He learned to use his computer and his printer quickly, learning MS Word, Gmail and Facebook in his seventies. With his newly learned skill, he encoded most of the school documents by himself.

His involvement with education prompted Felipe R. Verallo Foundation College, Bogo Cebu to grant him a Master of Arts in Education, *honoris causa.*

April 5, 2000, accompanied by my parents, I walked up the stage of the Cultural Center of the University of San Carlos, South Campus to get my rolled up symbolic diploma—the real one had to be requested from school a few weeks later—for my Doctorate of Philosophy in Education. Fr. Roderick Salazar—daddy's very distant cousin— with other school dignitaries, stood in the middle of the stage with my diploma on his left hand and an eager right hand to do the handshake.

"Dô, kanus-a ka moeskwela ani?" (When are you you going to study for this?) Fr. Salazar asked daddy with a tone of familiarity having had several school head conferences together.

"Hapit na." (Soon.) Daddy replied sheepishly.

Originally, it was not in his plan to take up a doctorate degree but being the school president, he felt obliged to take it, especially that his eldest daughter already had one. A few years later he enrolled and attended classes for his Doctor of Organization Development in School Administration at the Cebu Doctor's University. He even asked me for a copy of my dissertation as a guide for his. A few years later we celebrated this achievement with a family dinner.

Through the 'Expanded Teritary Education Equivalent Accreditation Program (ETEEAP), daddy was also given the degree of Doctor in Management by the University of the Visayas.

Daddy was willing to learn something novel. He self-studied to complete either a Maritime Transportation or the Marine Engineering program. The only requirement missing was the apprenticeship onboard a ship.

"I have studied all the courses for the maritime program. All I need to do is to ride a boat," he boasted to me while I sat in front of him in his office.

He was so confident of himself that before the turn of the 21st century, he applied, and was accepted, to be part of the *Who's Who* book in America, *a biographical dictionary of notable living men and women. He also applied, and was accepted, for a scholarship at the University of Hawaii in the 70s. Since he was at the peak of his career at that time—having numerous construction projects all over the Philippines—he postponed his scholarship for three years until he decided to give it up. I couldn't imagine life in Hawaii, had daddy accepted the scholarshhip.*

Here's another one of Tiya Jean's story during one of those daily bike trips to school with daddy biking and Tiya Jean backriding...

"Katsila, maka drive kog sakyanan nga wala pa koy traynta." [*Katsila*, (Spanish—Tiya Jean had Spanish features) I will be driving a car before I reach thirty.] Thirteen years later he showed up with a jeep!

"Ingon ka nga una ka mag traynta naa kay sakyanan? Jeep man lagi na!" (You told me that you were going to get a car before you turned 30? Instead you showed me a jeep!'), Tiya Jean jokingly pointed out.

A week later, he traded it in for a *used green car*! He kept his promise at the age of 29!

While he soared academically, he equally excelled in sports, just like in his high school days! The CIT college basketball team regarded him as an exceptional point guard. He was a champion marathon runner in Leyte and Cebu.

"I run faster without shoes," daddy told Adam. Daddy ran in his bare feet to give him more traction and speed. It also lengthened the life of his expensive shoes.

When I was in high school, daddy showed me how to play tennis in our very own tennis court, in front of our three-bedroom concrete beach house in Pooc, Talisay, the next town south of Cebu City.

"This is how you hold the ball." (daddy's term for the tennis shuttlecock, holding it high above his head)

"Then you stand like this." (feet apart with the left foot in front of the right foot) "and your other hand like this." (his right hand holding the tennis racquet, lifted high above his head, in a side stride, to give the racquet the perfect spot to hit the ball).

I wasn't very good at sports, but his training made me a referee in our college badminton game.

As an avid tennis player, he practiced batting every morning in our garage at our Guadalupe home. He painted a very-well-calculated line on the garage wall, to simulate a tennis net sagging at the middle.

When he did not play tennis, he lifted weights. Not the usual dumbbells that you order from *Amazon*, but home-made dumbbells. He filled two large empty paint cans with cement and stuck a piece of galvanized metal water pipe through the cement-filled cans. Although he was making millions (in Philippines pesos) by that time, he still used his ingenuity and resourcefulness to create something from whatever recycled materials we had. Since the storage area behind our garage was full of recycled construction materials, he had lots to choose from.

Since daddy was a man full of intelligence, humor and guts, Tiyo Boy (mommy's first cousin), played matchmaker with him. Tiyo Boy was daddy's classmate in freshman Algebra in CIT. Seeing daddy's brilliance in Algebra, Tiyo Boy, together with his close friends-classmates, sought daddy's help to tutor them in Algebra. Daddy made Algebra sound so easy for them.

While in Cebu, Tiyo Boy lived with his parents in their home on Don Pedro Cui, a few streets at the back of Cebu Normal College, mommy's alma mater. Tiyo Boy thought that daddy's brilliance in math would complement mommy's socialite character. He wanted daddy to be part of his family. Since mommy boarded with Tiyo Boy's family, it was natural for him to help mommy find a suitable partner.

This could have been a possible scenario:

Dô, naa koy guapa nga ig-agaw nga akong ipa-ilaila nimo. (Dô, I have a pretty cousin that I want you to meet.)

Mao ba? Sige kanus-a man? (Really! Ok when can I meet her?)

Sa sunod nga sayaw ni Naiding sa iyang eskwelahan. (At Naiding's next school dance.)

Throughout the remaining of their college years—and beyond—daddy and mommy became inseparable.

He had a choice though. While he dated mommy, he also dated *Mejing*, the daughter of a rich rancher from Mindoro. When Tiya Jean and her siblings asked him whom he was going to marry, he said that he would rather marry mommy, not just because he loved her more but also because he wanted to get the credit, in case they got rich after marriage.

*Siblings celebrating mass in honor of their parents at the Salazar Shrine
(constructed by daddy). Gakat, Southern Leyte. November 7, 2011.*

*Mini Salazar reunion (with their spouses), Notice how different daddy looks since
his 2011 picture with his siblings. Gakat, Southern Leyte. May 25, 2016.*

Genesis 2:18 (ESV)

Then the LORD God said, "It is not good that the man
should be alone; I will make him a helper fit for him."

Three

Where's the Disco?

Together with our school consultants, Adam and I went to Manila around the end of May 2022, to submit documents needed for certain school inspections. Since daddy passed away on July 23, 2017, Adam was first in line to succeed on the *throne*. Not only was he the eldest son, but he was also dad's choice. Being a year younger than Adam, and the only professional teacher among the siblings, I naturally helped him with the school.

While we planned to join the pinning, capping, badging, and candle lighting ceremony for our first year nursing students at Sacred Heart Center, we missed the event. Our flight from Manila was delayed for several hours. Mommy and her two helpers attended without us. Unlike her usual behaviour of sitting onstage and being in the limelight, she preferred to sit among the participants. She didn't even eat that night. She only had her favorite coke.

Adam and I arrived from Manila late Saturday night. I felt a bit guilty for not being with mommy for that important occasion. The next morning, I waited for mommy at the breakfast table at around 8am but the helper said that she still did not want to get up. Lunch came yet she refused to get up. I was really worried since she usually joined me for meals. By 2pm I told the helper to encourage mommy to come down. While I had my afternoon snacks, mommy sat across me at the dining table. She only had two bites of rice and fish when she started to gag and spit out the partly-chewed food. She waved her hand to her caregivers implying that she wanted to go back to bed. She stayed in bed without dinner.

After two days in bed without a decent meal, I called a doctor for a house visit. The doctor recommended that mommy be confined in the hospital for further check up. Since mommy refused to go on her own, I requested Sir Stephen, a school instructor, and head nurse, emergency department, at Cebu Doctor's Hospital, to encourage her to get admitted. Incidentally, he had to carry her to the car, against her will. Both Sir Stephen and Maam Carol, Dean of our College of Nursing, attended to mommy's first few hours at the emergency department of Cebu Doctor's Hospital. Those three weeks in the hospital were critical. We siblings thought that she wouldn't make it home. But God had His plan.

Before she went home, we decided to convert the formal dining room into her personal suite. A quick renovation of the room was done. It included painting, improving light fixtures, installing wall-to-wall curtains, removing the broken chadelier, and installing a big screen television on the wall, across her hospital bed (borrowed from the school's Nursing Skills Laboratory). The china cabinets were emptied of dinnerware, silverware, and everything else used for special dinners. They were replaced by mommy's personal stuff. Finally, a single bed for a newly-hired live-in professional caregiver was made available. The two helpers were still available to assist the caregiver.

From then on, life for mommy was focused on taking her medication and doing her regular exercises to strengthen her arms and leg muscles. The hired physical therapist encouraged her to walk with a cane, unassissted. There was a time when she was even able to walk for a few steps on her own, unassisted. Holding tight on the wooden handrail, she was also able to climb up the seven steps to her old bedroom.

A year later, April 17, 2023, mommy's blood pressure went up and her oxygen level went down, below the 90 mark. Xrays revealed that she had *penumonia in both lungs*. A week after she was confined, I didn't have a good night's sleep. At first I was reluctant to come home from Canada, since I was scheduled to visit her for the whole month of June.

"…make plans…Mommy unconscious *na (already)*", Adam's message stared at me when I read it on my phone at 5:30 the morning of April 24, Monday.

I felt like a ton of rock pounded on my heart. But I still got ready for my 7am shift. After I had a quick breakfast, I paused and prayed for wisdom. If I stayed, I would have many more sleepless nights. If I went I would be spending beyond our budget but I would be able touch, talk, and see mommy…for the very last time. Most of all, I would be able to spend time with my siblings, family and friends when the time came for her to go and funeral arrangements be made.

Right after chatting with Adam, I sent a text message to my boss saying that I had to go home (to Cebu) that day. With very limited choices, I opted to buy a really expensive ticket (Cdn$ 5,496.26)—more than three times my usual fare. It was the fastest route home. I quickly switched my uniform into my traveling attire and packed lightly.

Spending the first night at our Guadalupe home, I visited mommy in her private room in Chong Hua the following day. She had a mask on, which was connected to medical equipments to assist her breathe. It was reminiscent of my last hospital visit with daddy.

Her eyes opened slightly and her head nodded a bit when I called…

"Mommy! I'm here!", I greeted her cheerfully.

I asked the caregiver a few questions then I looked at her frail hands and socked feet. Her long fingernails were devoid of manicure. I removed her long white socks and checked her toenails. When I checked her warm sole for any abnormal marks, she quickly wiggled her feet and pulled it slightly closer to her body.

"You want your socks off 'My (mommy)?", I asked her with amusement. Frowning, she shook her head as if to tell me to put her socks back on. I knew she always wanted to keep her feet warm. As soon as I put back her socks, she settled down. She was still conscious after all.

On April 26, 2023, Wednesday, at around 5:35pm, I visited mommy. Grace, our Christian working student and househelper, and I took turns reading the scripture:

> John 3:16 "For God so loved the world, that he gave his only Son, that whoever believes in him should not perish but have eternal life."

> Revelation 21:4 "He will wipe away every tear from their eyes, and death shall be no more, neither shall there be mourning, nor crying, nor pain anymore, for the former things have passed away."

I prayed with her the sinner's prayer. She was already non-responsive but I knew that she still heard me. I told her to pray this sinner's prayer with me, "Lord forgive my sins. I accept you as my Lord and Saviour who forgives my sins and takes me to eternal life. In Jesus name, amen". I also told her that if she wanted to see me and daddy in heaven, that she have Faith in Jesus so that her sins will be forgiven then the Lord will take her to heaven after she passed. [I also prayed this prayer with daddy, a few days before he passed on July 23, 2017.]

"Mommy you can go now. Don't worry about us, we will take care of ourselves," I told her, weeping. It was an emotional moment.

An hour later, her condition deteriorated rapidly. Coincidence? God's providence.

Her oxygen level went down to the 80s, for five minutes, despite having an oxygen mask. Rita, the caregiver on duty, notified the nurses at the station of her condition. Two nurses came to remove saliva from her mouth. Then they suctioned phlegm from her throat. Inspite of that procedure, her oxygen level had remained below the normal level.

Her lungs were really in a bad shape. The oxygen monitor kept on beeping for at least 16 minutes. And then her blood pressure went down to 70-40. Through various interventions, the doctors tried their best to keep her blood pressure and oxygen at their best levels. After three days, without much improvement, the family and doctors agreed to give her the best quality of life, with the least pain.

We siblings were more proactive this time around. We had a feeling that her soul was leaving soon. Several hours before her passing, my siblings were able to transfer funds, locate her memorial plan, and have funeral arrangements ready.

I arrived around 8:30pm on the 28th of April after a long day in school. Family was around as we noticed her breathing intervals were getting longer... and longer..... until it stopped.

She was called home, at 8:56pm.

As soon as she left, I placed my hands on her warm chest to feel the heat of her love and embrace, allowing her to go—to turn pale, to turn cold and rigid—then I said good-bye... in silence.

A few minutes later, the nurse came with an equipment to check her heart beat. It beeped and showed a long flat line. A single line showing the end of her physical presence with us, the line confirming that we were orphans. No mommy. No daddy. Only adult children fending for ourselves. I felt a void, an emptiness. Ultimate realization of being alone.

Eleven days after she was confined, she breathed her last. I did not regret coming home. My presence meant a lot to mommy and to my family. No amount of money could ever buy this.

Her passing was not as tragic sa daddy's since she had shown weakness for a year. Daddy's passing rehearsed us for mommy's. Her wake was held at the Our Lady of China Chapel, beside Sacred Heart Church, the very same chapel where daddy had his week-long wake.

Mommy's wake was for only two days. Daddy had half a day viewing in school while mommy was brought straight to the chapel. Mommy's well-wishers were only about a third of daddy's. While the future Cebu City Mayor Michael Rama visited daddy during his wake, Madridejos Mayor Romeo Villaceran, with his wife Violy, and their Councilors attended mommy's wake.

Among the other well-wishers during both wakes were members of the immediate family, relatives from the Salazar and Figuracion clans, friends, neighbors, and past and present employees, students, and the medical team with their families and friends.

Was daddy more popular than mommy? No doubt daddy was the orator, the voice of the family, while mommy was the *iron woman behind the voice*. The woman who made daddy who he was, who loved and cared for him until his last day on earth. The woman who gave daddy six children, nineteen grandkids, and six great grand kids!

Fr. Randy condensed mommy's character during his sermon in the Mass at mommy's wake. She was a *Negotiator, Artistic, Intimidating, Disciplinarian, Industrious, Nurturer, and a Gift from God*.

Negotiator. She negotiated deals with a "Take it or Leave it" attitude. Haggling prices from poor sidewalk vendors gave her a thrill. Saving P5-10 (US$ 0.09-0.18) from a P160.00 (US$ 2.87) per kilo of mangoes made her day. She expected her staff to haggle for prices too. She was so desperate to save every centavo she could.

Artistic. Mommy was an artist. During the prime of her life, she never left home without make-up, jewelry, and matching outfit (including shoes, bag, and accessories). She also made sure that daddy's outfit matched hers.

Absolutely gorgeous!

A picture with their parents and in-laws just in the living room of our Labangon home before coronation night of "Reyna sa San Nicholas" (Queen of San NIcholas Parish). My parents are wearing a Muslim-inspired outfits. Cebu City. September 1968.

Mommy, as the "Reyna sa San Nicholas", was crowned by a politician, Benigno "Ninoy" Aquino, and a celebrity, Pilar Pilapil. A third of my body shows on the right. San Nicholas Parish, Cebu City. September 1968.

Mommy's presence commanded full respect. Cebu City. Early 80s. (photo credit: Chris Odtohan)

Her artistic nature was reflected in the house décor, garden arrangement, and the helpers' uniforms. The Royal family's lifestyle must have had a huge influence on her. No wonder furnishing from scenes of *The Crown*, a Netflix series, reminds me so much of the furnishings of our Guadalupe home.

Intimidating. This is an understatement of mommy! She was a *tiger*! (as her former staff and helpers used to call her). She *growled* when she got upset! *Never come close to mommy when she was in this mood.* Daddy knew that. We siblings knew that.

Everyone knew that. The trick was to remember all the instructions she gave and do them when it was needed to be done. Simple. Another trick was not to take it personally. It was just her job to put everything in order. *Everything!* From her six kids (and the household helpers, house boy, drivers, and security guards) to their many businesses (including clients, suppliers, engineers, foremen, laborer, teachers, office staff, working students, drivers, shop mechanics, and many more). She made sure that there was enough resources to keep each one of them going.

Mommy set herself up on a pedestal making sure that everyone respected her for who she was. She was a perfectionist and a goal-getter. No one could stop her.

Disciplinarian. As Comander-in-Chief of her life (and the lives of others), it was natural for mommy to make sure that her instructions were followed *verbatim*. She expected her staff to be fast learners. Nothing upset her more than slow learners and slowpokes. With an extremely busy lifestyle, she was annoyed by repeating instructions over and over again. She and daddy were constantly on hectic schedules that anything short of perfection triggered her *inner volcano*, ready to burst at the first person she saw! Ready to correct errors instantly (with demeaning words).

She discplined me too. Whenever I made my younger siblings cry (for not sharing toys with them), I was made to kneel on sea salt, with both arms raised sideward while facing a corner of our Labangon home, for about 10-15 minutes!

When I turned 19, a sophomore college student, I was still disciplined. I was attending a week-long live-in leadership convention with almost a hundred international AIESEC members, at a well-known university in Manila. On the last night, I was surpised to see our driver outside our plenary hall during coffee break! He said that mommy instructed him to pick me up so that I would spend the night at our Cubao home. I was furious! I wanted to spend more time mingling with my new friends! After a few hours of more fun and laughter over training sessions, dinner, and after dinner snacks, I packed up my belongings. I informed my Malaysian roommates that I was spending the night at home. I felt obliged to follow mommy's instructions since I did not want to get a *hurricane scolding* once I reached Cebu.

I was *the* only delegate who spent the last night outside of the venue. I reached home at about 10pm to meet our househelper who asked me if I wanted something to eat. How could I have an appetite when all I wanted was to be with my friends? I went straight to bed, helpless. The following day, breakfast was served early in the morning. Again without any appetite to eat, I told the driver to drive me back to my seminar-workshop. The last day of the workshop was spent listening to the fun stories I missed attending. As I look back at that time today, I realize that mommy was just trying to protect me from whatever harm she thought could have happened to me as a teenager.

Industrious. Mommy's (and daddy's) day started with 7am breakfast with all her children at the table and the helpers waiting by the side of the kitchen. As soon as the driver left with the family van at 7:15am, dropping us at our private schools, mommy and daddy headed for the office. These were the 70s and 80s when it only took 15-20 minutes to commute from home to school. By 11:30am, the driver picked us up from school to have lunch at home with my parents. By 1pm, off we went back to school. By 4:30-5:30 he would pick us up to join them again for dinnertime. On Saturdays, they left an hour or two later depending on how meticulous mommy's instructions were for the househelpers. Saturdays were focused on garden maintenance and groceries. Mommy was just as hard-working as daddy. Running family businesses wasn't easy.

Nurturer. Sundays were family days. Mommy made it a point that everyone went to church on Sundays and then to the beach after—to Pook, Talisay when we were little, and later to Punta Engaño (when Talisay was no longer ideal for swimming).

On occasional Saturdays we had dinner out at any of their favorite Chinese restaurants (Majestic Restaurant, Great Han Palace or White Gold House). As we got older and busier, we skipped going to the beach but we enjoyed dinners at Casino Español, while our children swam in the pool, played bowling, or simply enjoyed the company of the family and occasional guests. Mommy made sure that we were well fed. She was not very affectionate but she supplied us with enough materials things.

Mommy was also nurturing to our extended family. She provided housing (with minimal fees) to Jaures and many members of the Figuracion clan. Through mommy's help, Jaures was able to finish college, get a job, and eventually settle done in the US. Mommy also provided supporting documents to Lola Monda, in the mid 80s. Her case was more complicated.

Lola Monda, mommy's distant aunt, was born in Hawaii, as a daughter of a *sakada* (migrant farmworker) father. When life in the Hawaian pineapple plantation was unbrearable to a four year old, Lola's father decided to come home to Madridejos bringing lola with him and leaving lola's older sister and their mother in Hawaii. Lola grew up in Madridejos and married Lolo Edel. They had seven children. Mommy learned about Lola Monda's story when Lolo Edel and Boy Terok (one of the couple's sons) became the trusted painters of the carozza used for the Holy Week procession. Seeing the family in poverty, mommy encouraged Lola Monda to regain her US Citizenship so that their living conditions would be better. After a lot of family discussions, document preparation, and interviews, lola was able bring her family to the US. Through mommy's gracious gestures, several family members were able to have better lives in the Philippines and abroad.

Gift from God. No double mommy was a gift from God, a gift wrapped in *tiger skin*, but she meant well. Some family members, former employees and friends may not see her inner beauty since she oftentimes looked aloof. She was terribly *tihik* (stingy) too, limiting food and other resources at hand. Whenever we had breakfast at mommy's house, Jun, my husband used to say, *"Maka-on nako ang tanang pagkaon diha sa lamesa nga giandam ni mommy para sa walo!"* (I can eat all those food prepared by mommy for eight!).

When I had children of my own, mommy invited our family for dinner, and I had to bring a helper or two with me, to watch my little kids. She would ask each one of us what we wanted to have for dinner, skipping the question for the helpers. Their dinner was skipped too. There were the few times when I had to ask extra plates for our helpers. But mommy made sure that the helper got the less expensive meal.

During the early years of the business, when family members helped, their food allowances and food rations were also limited. My kids and their cousins experienced the *ultimate diet* with their *mama*, a single adult size hamburger was split into four, for four grandkids. After each kid finish their *kid-size burger*, mommy had them finish a banana.

During those times it was difficult to see how she was a gift to us. Gifts are expected to be pleasant, but she *seemed* otherwise. Nevertheless, all of her was still a gift to us. She touched our lives in many ways.

Did she have a difficult childhood? What was mommy's upbringing? What brought her to seek the life of luxury and yet stay stingy? Or did her stinginess help her achieve our family wealth?

Born Zenaida *Naiding* Montaño Figuracion on April 23, 1935, in Madridejos, Cebu, mommy was the eldest child of Mr. Justiniano *Justin* Tiongzon Figuracion, a farmer-turned politician, and Mrs. Bebiana *Bibing* Almodiel Montaño, a fish dealer. I fondly call them Lolo Usting and Lola Bibing.

She graduated from grade six at Madridejos Central Elementary School—whose early years was interrupted by the Second World War—and high school at Madridejos Provincial High School (now named Madridejos National High School).

As the eldest of six siblings, mommy supervised her younger siblings, while Lolo Usting tended to their farm in Tugas and Pili, and Lola Bibing minded their fishing business. Lola Bibing had a large *basnigan* (fishing vessel), named Zenaida, which had a a fisher crew of about 30. They had two pump boats, JUBE 1 and JUBE 2, (for Justin and Bebing).

At a young age mommy was *house manager*, telling her younger siblings to do household chores including babysitting their youngest sister. There were times, however, when Lolo Usting asked mommy and her siblings to help in the farm and in the fishing business. They had no choice but to help out, otherwise lolo did not give them their allowance. No work. No allowance.

Lola Bibing had pump boats similar to the one above. Ritz continued lola's legacy by naming his pump boat "JUBIE" after her pump boats. This is the actual 'baybay'(beach front) across mommy's ancestral home, Madridejos, Cebu. 2022.

Mommy developed a strong work ethic early in life, especially from Lolo Usting, the original *tihik* patriarch of the family. Ritz, my first cousin, told me that one of mommy's jobs at the farm was to bring the cows to the grassland (*magtogway sa baka*). He heard a lot of stories about mommy from Lola Bibing since he spent his early childhood with her and Lolo Usting in Madridejos.

When mommy was in her early teens, she also went with Lola Bibing to sell dried fish in local markets at various towns of Cebu during *tabô* (market days).

After high school, mommy crossed the seas to finish her Bachelor of Elementary Education at the Cebu Normal College (Cebu Normal University). Her morena complexion, her lovely smile, and her elegant poise caught the attention of her teachers as she was asked to join the school's beauty contest. She was either *Miss Education* or *Miss Cebu Normal College,* while still a freshman.

Mommy (leftmost) met daddy (rightmost) during her college years at Cebu Normal College. Photographs had jagged edges then. Mid 50s.

My parents attended the college graduation of Tiyo Titing (one of the twin brothers of mommy) at the Cebu Normal College. Tiyo Titing is flanked by his parents, Lola Bebing and Lolo Usting. Standing behind them (left to right) are Tiyo Abring, mommy, daddy, and Tiyo Toto. Cebu. 1963. (photo credit: L.F.J.)

After mommy's graduation in 1957, she taught in several public schools including Sulangan Elementary School, Bantayan, Cantabaco Elementary School, Toledo City (in 1959 after her marriage), Buhisan and Labangon Elementary Schools (both in Cebu City).

Graduate of Bachelor in Elementary Education.
Cebu Normal College Cebu, 1957.

Among her colleagues at Labangon Elementary School, Cebu City. 1967-1968.

While she did well as a public school teacher, daddy's construction business needed more help. Out of many discussions with daddy, she finally resigned from her teaching job to help him in his business.

Mommy's role in daddy's business was crucial. She made sure that funds were collected and directed to where they were needed, at the right time. Although she did not have formal training in finance or accounting, she knew exactly where the funds were coming from and which expense needed to be spent on what day.

A visit from Sayo, her future Japanese granddaugther-in-law, Sayo's mom, and Anthony. There's a can of 'M.Y. San Assorted Biscuits' on the floor and a candy jar on mommy's table. Those were her staples for mid-day snacks. All paperwork was done by hand, without using the calculator or computer. Daddy's table, on the right, was within arms reach. June 2009.

She admitted to me, just a few years before she passed, that she did not even know how to use the calculator. Her celphone was the ancient Nokia model. Growing up before the age of the internet, Facebook, Gmail, or Microsoft Office, she found technology too complicated. She refused to learn something new. She didn't need to. She had her loyal staff to do her books, her way! They were just a buzzer away.

She requested one of our carpenters to attach a buzzer to the right side of her office table. Whenever she needed anything from the finance staff, she buzzed them according to their codes. Then in they came with logbooks or folders full of receipts and yellow pads showing the lists she needed. She checked them page and page and signed them at the end of each page. She had a unique way of keeping track of income and expenses. She used the *tinamban* (extrapolating) style of accounting where figures were rounded off and remembered keenly. And computer print outs were not needed.

On one home visit, mommy wanted me to be familiar with the finances of our businesses. She asked me to check pages and pages of handwritten dates, numbers and asked me to sign at the bottom of each page. I could not make sense of them! I wanted to see Financial Statements and Ratios and other professional things I learned at business school. But there was nothing she could show me. I had to talk to our internal and external Auditors to find out the real picture. She was truly street smart with numbers!

She was so careful about spending that she even removed tips daddy placed on dinner tables. She was so cautious with cash outflows and excellent with cash inflows.

"Mommy was the recycle queen!", Adam said at her wake.

Even before anyone thought about recycling (newspapers, bottles, paint cans, scrap metal, plastic, sacks of rice, sacks of cement...) she had been doing it since the 60s. She asked the helpers and construction workers to gather recyclable items so that they can be turned into cash from the Taboan buyers. She was very environment friendly!

Our rental properties used recycled construction materials whenever possible. Mommy joined daddy visiting construction sites. While daddy talked to the foremen and construction crew about engineering designs, mommy reminded them to sort unused materials for recyling.

Mommy seemed to fear the shortage of money. She must have had traumatic early childhood experiences with hunger, difficulty obtaining cash or the necessities of life which must have unconsciously motivated her to be prudent about her resources.

In the early 70s, when daddy had a multi-million construction project in Manila, I overheard their staff say that we almost got bankrupt. I was only ten years old then but I recall vividly that our family (with our nannies) spent the whole summer in a rented apartment in Quezon City so that my parents were able to focus on their project. I recall the heated conversations daddy had with his construction lead men about how things had to be done. On our way to a family dinner on a Saturday afternoon, daddy drove the family car—with mommy, our nannies and six kids inside—through the construction site. He stopped beside the Lead Foreman and gave him last minute instructions.

"*Kinahanglan buhaton na nga dili pa mahuman ang adlaw!*"(That had to be done before the day ends!)

They must have pulled through since our construction business kept on going after that project was completed. My business teachers shared that "Out of ten businesses, one business fails." I am very sure that my parents were aware of that. While daddy was winning bids in construction projects, mommy was scrimping (*nanaginot*), a negative sounding word but it was a golden virtue.

Another golden trait was organizing her day. She kept on reminding her workers on a daily basis of the things that needed to be done. As early as 6:30 in the morning, she would call the helpers' names one by one for them to come to her bedroom door to receive their instructions for the day. In our huge home, she had to use her *loud Commander voice* to summon them to come.

Ninfa, niay kwarta palit manga, puto, ug sikwate! (Ninfa, here is cash to buy mango, sticky rice, and Filipino hot chocolate!)

Ibon, andama ang uniporme sa mga bata! (Yvonne, please prepare the uniforms of the children.

Jobing, pagda ug init tubig sa kwarto! [Jobing, please bring hot water (in a pail) to our room.]

They did not have electric water heater then. Our helpers had to boil water in a kettle and pour them in a pail. By the way, Jobing (Tiya Jobing) is mommy's first cousin. She, like a few of my relatives, lived with us and was given household jobs, in exchange for a free living expenses and a college education.

Before mommy left for the office daily there was a litany of reminders...

"*Bisbisi ang tanum, guntingi ang mga balili, silhigi ang mga kwarto, pagmop sa sawog. Inig panihapun pagluto ug tinowa ug pritong isda, unya paghimo og salad nga camote tops. Inita ang mga sud-an sa kagabii.*"

(Water the plants, cut the grass, sweep the rooms, mop the floor. Then at dinnertime, cook fish soup and fried fish, then prepare salad from the newly sprouted leaves of the sweet potato plants. Reheat the leftovers from last night). Her distinctively strict voice echoed through our mansion. It served as my annoying alarm clock on Saturday mornings. I miss her voice. It reminded me of how meticulous she was with daily routine.

Since she and daddy had their businesses in the early 60s she always observed a 9-6 office hours, including a three-hour lunch/*siesta* (mid-day nap) break.

After daddy passed mommy was more involved with the school. It was good enough if she went to the office and sat in her office chair, an hour in the morning and an hour in the afternoon.

She watched TV, ate either cookies or *bananaque* (deep-fried saba banana skewered onto a barbeque stick and coated in caramelized brown sugar) together with a small bottle of Coke. When drivers were available, she went church hopping on Wednesdays or Fridays, to light candles (or have her caregivers light for her), and when able, she attended Mass at the Basílica Minore del Santo Niño de Cebú.

Her yearly Madridejos trips became more frequent. She prefered to stay at Cottage 2 in her beachside Tarong property. Lighting a candle at Immaculate Conception Parish Church (the church she and daddy renovated) and speaking *Lawisanun* to family and friends around the church pleased her.

What pleased her most was dancing to the tune of the original version of *chacha, tango, and boogie*!

"Where's the disco?", mommy asked Adam, who hurriedly called Tibor to set-up the sound system, called the teachers and staff of SCSIT Madridejos campus for her dancing partners, and had an instant disco party that night!

"I want the original chacha only!", as mommy added further instructions.

April 5th, 2023 was her last *baile* (dance)… after years of dancing at the Madridejos plaza as a young girl, or during parties with daddy, or with friends in the custom-made dance studio above the garage of our ancentral home. She just loved to dance, so much that she hired a *bayot DI* (gay Dance Instructor) to teach daddy how to dance, during her Cebu Normal days. She wanted daddy to be her dancing partner so he needed to step up!

(Above) An evening in Tiyo Boy's place, Cebu City, 2014.

Now she's dancing happily in heaven… eternally.

All of mommy's six siblings were complete during the Figuracion Clan reunion. (L-R, from the eldest to the youngest) mommy, Tiyo Abring, Tiyo Totong and Tiyo Titing (twins), Tiyo Toto, and Tiya Nene. SCSIT Madridejos Campus, Cebu. April 2014. (photo credit: L.F.J.)

Psalm 149:3 (ESV)

Let them praise his name with dancing, making melody to him with tambourine and lyre!

Four

Room for 6

Do you, Doroteo, take, Zenaida, as your lawfully wedded wife, to have and to hold from this day forward, for better or for worse, for richer, for poorer, in sickness and in health, to love and to cherish; from this day forward until death do you part?

I do.

Do you, Zenaida, take, Doroteo, as your lawfully wedded husband, to have and to hold from this day forward, for better or for worse, for richer, for poorer, in sickness and in health, to love and to cherish; from this day forward until death do you part?

I do.

Dodo, you may kiss your bride.

No mountains or seas separated the lovers. The Salazar family crossed the Camotes Sea—from Sogod, Leyte, to Cebu island, hopped on a ferry to Bantayan island, with several road trips in between—to meet the Figuracion clan in Madridejos.

Marriage vows were exchanged on July 25, 1959, Madridejos, Cebu.

Daddy and mommy tied the knot on July 25, 1959 at the Immaculate Conception Parish Church, Madridejos, Cebu. It was attended by family and friends on both sides. Majority of the guests were mommy's.

Lolo Nene, Lola Tonyay, and Tiya Inday were there, with a few other family members, to accompany daddy on this maiden voyage to the island of Bantayan. Tiya Inday was in charge of baking the lovely *three-tier wedding cake.*

When it was time to serve the cake, she couldn't get rid of those large black flies (*lagong* in Cebuano) hovering over the cake—take note Bantayan is the haven for dried fish and large black flies. They became *instant raisins* for the guests.

After the rings were exchanged, and other wedding rituals finished, the couple decide to settle in Cebu City, renting a tiny one bedroom place across Lolo Dodong's.

My parents were happy and excited to start their lives together. Here is the wedding cake Tiya Inday made. Madridejos, Cebu. July 25, 1959.

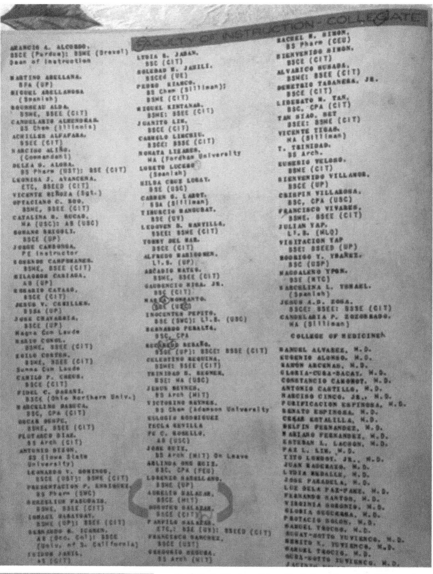

Both Lolo Dodong (Aurelio Salazar) and daddy taught at the Cebu Institute of Technology (CIT) College of Engineering. Lolo Dodong graduated Civil Engineering at the Mapúa Institute of Technology (MIT). (taken from the CIT yearbook 'Residuum' 1959, a copy daddy kept at the basement office at our Guadalupe home)

The CIT College Yearbook.

The gentleman with the widest smile, in white shoes, is my dad (tenth seated person from the right.) Cebu Institute of Technology. 1961.

Children came very soon after. I arrived exactly one year and sixteen days after Adam was born.

Two adults, an infant, and a toddler became too many for a one-bedroom pad. The young and ambitious couple, daddy (23) and mommy (24), vowed to build a house of their own. Although their place was conveniently located in the downtown core—where they could easily grab a *jeepney* or a *tartanilla*, or buy their groceries in *Pasil* and *Taboan* (wet markets)—their very own home was still much better.

To maintain our home, and increasing expenses, my parents needed much more than their combined monthly paychecks of *less than P400.00 (US $7.20) a month.*

After a few years of teaching at the College of Engineering at CIT, daddy grabbed the chance to start his Salazar Construction firm. His first project was to build a fence around a friend's house. Simple, yet a promising start to being his own boss. His track record at CIT paved the way to being awarded the construction project of the second CIT campus on C. Padilla Street (presently occupied by Don Carlos A. Gothong Memorial High School).

Borrowing money from Lolo Usting and Lola Bibing (from a loan of their farm lands) and recruiting family members and a few hired hands, they were able to have extra income to purchase a piece of land for a future home.

600-J Tres de Abril Street, Labangon, Cebu City
….the site of our future school.

My parents with their first two children, Adam and myself.
I was just eleven months old. January 1962.

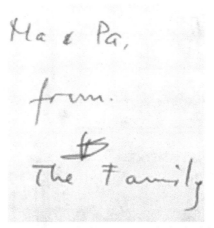

Daddy's handwritten message for his parents at the back of the photo above.

January 1962—a month short of my first birthday— was the date I saw on the white border of a black and white photo of our two story wooden house. The same construction crew who made the CIT project built our very first home.

"It was your daddy's blood, sweat and tears." Tiya Jean messaged me on Facebook's Messenger.

(Above) Stairs leading to my parents' room on the left of the landing and the room of the last three siblings on the right of the landing. The two elder girls' room were at the basement. The oldest boy's room was across these rooms. Labangon, Cebu City, 1962.

Our formal dining rooms for guests only.

One of my favorite pastimes as a little girl was selling pretend candies—sun-dried *caimito* seeds (spat out on the ground by anyone in the household, while eating fresh *caimito* fruits) wrapped in used notebook paper. I pretended selling them to my little sisters. At times, we sold real candies, left over from daddy's *pasalubong* (souvenirs) from his occasional trips to Manila. In between our sale transactions, we ate a few pieces of the wrapped *durian* candy or the M&M.

Another favorite game was cooking *real rice* in three-inch clay pots [bought by *yayas* (nannies) in *Taboan*] and using dried leaves and twigs lit with a matchstick, snatched from our kitchen. Boy, that smell of burnt rice was good! We didn't eat it, we just loved the idea of cooking our own food, as a game of pretend cooking! Mommy didn't know that we *played* with rice. Filipino culture frowns on anyone playing with real food because of the belief on *gaba* (negative karma).

A home-made cement *aquarium*—complete with red, blue, and green lights—was built under the landing of the main entrance door of the house. Originally real fish swam on both sides of the forked landing, sort of a moat. When the helpers could not take care of the fish, and they died a natural death, Cecile made it a dog den. She placed Johnson's baby powder on our native, unbathed, unvaccinated dogs and spent hours playing with them, and even took afternoon naps with them. No wonder daddy called her *Dudug*.

Bad Boy! He would call out for Adam. *Bad boy* fit as a pet name for Adam since he always teased his younger siblings.

Dy! (for daddy)

Abakating tungguy! He would be calling me.

Dy!

Dudug! and he would be calling out to Cecile.

Dy!

Whenever daddy came home, he would do a roll call of all his children, calling us by our pet names. (I just could not remember the pet names of my younger siblings.) I always grinned whenever he called me *Abakating tungguy!* I loved it! It didn't mean anything except that it showed daddy's love and affection to his children.

There were many ways daddy showed his affection to us. I was asked a few times to scratch his back with my tiny fingers, like a back scratcher. He would call me in the middle of his shower—in the only interior bathroom we had for the family—crouched down so that I could only see his back, then opens the door, and calls me.

"Abet scratch my back! Some more to the left and down and then up again.", daddy instructed me as I scratched his back like a bath sponge does.

During hot summer months daddy made home-made ice cream using a large bucket-size electric ice-cream machine. He placed milk, sugar, and fruits (depending on the availability) in the circular metal container in the middle of the bucket, surrounded by chunks of ice. A stirring device was attached to the handle, which churned the ingredients in the metal container for hours until ice cream was made. The loud noise of the ice cream machine excited us! As a child, I sat in front of the ice cream machine and waited until daddy served ice cream to me. It was a great summer treat!

In the cool months of December, daddy bought bags of *castañas* (chestnuts) imported from China, sold by street vendors in Colon Street. He stirred fried them in sand until they were slightly burned and roasted. He said that adding sand to the frying pan (*kahâ*)—chinese-wok-looking frying pan—increases the heat of the pan and cooks the chestnuts faster. That song *Chestnuts Roasting on an Open Fire* reminds me so much of daddy's *castañas*.

Our very own homegrown Christmas tree. This original design of the house did not have a forked landing or an aquarium by the front entrance. No air conditioning was used then. We just opened all the windows and doors to allow fresh air to come in. Early 60s.

A large tree stood in between the forked landing of our first house. Prior to a terrible storm, it was cut off to prevent it from landing on our roof. A rectangular baluster-lined porch was at the end of the left forked landing. Wavy orange and white square tiles, similar to the tiles in the living room, covered the porch floor. Rainy days left an inch or two of rain water on the porch floor, perfect for sliding on our bellies.

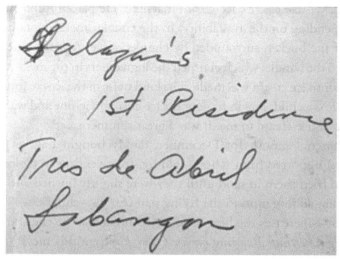

Mommy's handwritten message at the back of the picture of our first home.

There were days when I sat on the railing of the baluster, and watched mommy teach her fourth graders dance the *Cariñosa*— traditional dance of courtship in the colonial-era where a fan or handkerchief is used by the dancing couple. She gracefully showed her students the right steps, reminding them to smile with every movement.

As a teacher, mommy had occasional students and co-teachers visit her. The very-organized-and-neat mommy always reminded the helpers to keep the home, and it's surroundings, presentable. The front area of the house was always welcoming to guests.

When guests entered the front gate, they would see a metal double-bench swing at the left side. Grape vines grew on both sides of the front gate posts and behind the double-bench swing. A variety of flowers added color to the gardens in front and surrounding the house.

Tiya Jean poised on an iron patio chair by the front entrance garden. January 1965.

Our home's side and back gardens were full of *caimito, atis, tisa, balimbing, tambis, lomboy, mansanitas, siniguelas,* coconut, and other tropical fruit-bearing trees. It was like country living, in the middle of the city. When our dinner table, and our bellies, were full of fruits, the rest of the fruits fell off their branches to rot on the grounds. The seeds germinated naturally and grew into more trees.

Much of the action was at the back of the house. On boring weekends, I went out through our back door to watch the *labandera* (laundry woman) wash our clothes by hand, with the aid of a *batya* (large metal basin), and a *palo-palo* (flat, wooden washing paddle used as a laundry *dirt-buster*).

Daddy and mommy had a small cemented rectangular reservoir made for laundry purposes. It was a foot high, three feet long and two feet wide. During really hot summer days, my siblings and I converted this reservoir into *our swimming pool.* Using cool flowing tap water, we took lots of refreshing baths there!

Roses, roses, roses, my mom had a beautiful rose garden at the side of the house. We had rows and rows of potted rose plants—400 varieties of roses imported from Singapore through a supplier in the *Taboan* market. American-named, clay-potted rose plants were perfectly lined and placed on top of circular stone structures (made by one of daddy's cement masons). Each rose plant was properly labeled with its own metal handwritten name tags attached to its thorny stem. Saturday mornings was gardening time. I loved watching mommy show our helpers how to fertilize, spray with insecticides, prune, and marcot the plants. Their effort paid off. Soon enough mommy's friends and neighbors became her regular customers.

On the right side of her rose garden was a fish pond full of *carp, goldfish, rainbow fish,* tadpoles, frogs, and water lilies. Miniature sculptures of a fisherman and dwarves lined the fish pond.

After a few years, when too many frogs overcrowded the pond, it was converted into a *grotto*— Catholic shrine built with a rock formation.

My parents spent most of the 60s managing five children and extending help to uncles and aunties (on both sides). Cecile and I did not mind sharing our basement room with Tiya Jean, Auntie Flor, and Lola Tonyay (daddy's cousin, sister, and mom, respectively). Having roommates seemed to drive away the *mu-mûs* ("witches" from childhood tales).

Hala na-ay mu-mû diha! (Hey, there are witches there!)

Our yayas used to scare us, in the effort of making us stay close to them. We got so scared of the *mu-mûs* that we wanted someone to be beside us *all the time.*

Then there was Tiyo Ludy (daddy's sibling), Tiyo Abring, Tiyo Titing, Tiyo Totong, and Tiya Nene, (mommy's siblings), who became our housemates at home. Once in a while, Lola Bibing spent a few days with us, as a side trip, while consigning her dried fish in *Taboan.* Every time Lola Bibing came for a visit, she brought freshly fried *lagaw,* "bisugo" fish, wrapped in newspaper. We ate it straight from the newspaper. As the oldest granddaughter, I had the honor of looking for *white rabbit* candy— digging through receipts, paper lists, and pocketsize notebooks— in her black leatherette purse. Lola was fond of lending money to her fisherfolk employees, listing down the debts with very slim chance of repayment.

Between 1960-1971 daddy and mommy had six children: Adam, me, Cecile, Danielle, Eduardo, and Flint (aged 0 to 11). As the children and the housemates multiplied, so did our household helpers—from a single *yaya,* a *kusinera* (cook), and a *labandera* (laundry woman), to three yayas, a *kusinera,* a *labandera,* and a family driver.

Our garden walkways, on the northside of the home, were converted into bedrooms. Seeing that our home overflowed with people, cars, trucks, construction tools and equipment, our neighbors slowly approached my parents and offered to sell their properties (house and lot) to them—at very affordable prices and friendly terms.

My parents bought the ancestral home of Dionisio "Esyot" and Paz "Pasing" Aleria on the west side of our home, and the Ruiz property, on the east side. The Aleria's home became a boarding house for about thirty to forty engineering review students with Nang Lily and Nong Berto, her husband, as the official cook and caretaker.

I witnessed Nang Lily make *lumpia* (Filipino spring roll) wrapper from scratch. She whisked flour, egg, and water in a bowl, took a ladle-full of the white batter, and deftly poured it thinly into a hot pan for a minute or two. *Voilà!* Out came a wafer-thin *lumpia* wrapper—similar to crepes. It was amazing how they managed the kitchen, while her young children played around the kitchen area. She was an amazing cook, very cool-tempered, and worked round the clock.

While boarders were coming in and out of our adjacent boarding house, drivers from our passenger jeepneys came in and out of our home. By 1969, we had six passenger jeepneys traveling the Labangon-Carbon route, each one of them named after A to E with the sixth one named St. Joseph. (Flint was born the year after.)

Our house was one of the few decent houses in the neighborhood. Most of the surrounding houses used *nipa* (palm) leaves for roofs, ours was of G.I. sheets. Not only was our home different from our neighbors but our native tongue was also different— it was English— when mostly everyone else spoke Bisaya. In fact, all our household and office staff were requested to speak to us in English.

Daddy and mommy wanted to raise a family who would *fit with the English-speaking elite in the Philippine society*, in contrast to their less privileged backgrounds.

The Filipino culture has a distinct rich *elite* class and poor class, with very few members in the middle class. With majority of Filipinos living below the poverty line, the distinction can be seen in the type of home, choice of school, clothing, entertainment, language spoken at home, and the number or absence of private cars. No matter what class a Filipino belongs, every *pinoy* (how Filipinos called themselves) loves *everything* about America—food, fashion, Hollywood, and, most of all, the English language.

English-speaking Filipinos made heads turn in schools, offices, department stores, supermarkets, churches, parties, *everywhere*. English-speaking Filipinos seemed to belong to the few rich, the elite of the community, the entrepreneurs, the investors, the politicians, and the city-influencers, who easily closed deals with local and foreign investors.

My parents somehow foresaw that if they raised their children speaking in English, *this* universal language could give their children a chance to be at par with the rich Filipino, American, and Spanish *mestiza* and *mestizo* entrepreneurs in Cebu. Consequently, we were sent to private Catholic schools run by English-speaking priests or nuns .

I remember one time, when we didn't have classes, mommy brought Adam, Cecile, and me to Buhisan Elementary School, a public school located in the mountain slopes next to Labangon. Their school environment was very different from St. Theresa's College—my alma mater for 12 years. There was lots of plants and trees around the unlandscaped natural garden and uncemented pathways. Quite the opposite from the well-manicured lawns and all-cemented Theresian hallways and pathways. They had one storey wooden classrooms while our school had several 2-3 story cemented buildings.

My mom's students looked strangely at us. Was it because they saw their teacher's children for the first time? Or was it because we wore better clothes and shoes? And we spoke English?

When it was time to take our mid-day *siesta* (nap), mommy placed several two-seated wooden pews of her classroom, side by side, to make them like wooden beds. With light turned off, we lay down on top of them for about half an hour. I didn't nap. I couldn't. Not on the stiff wooden tables (without any pillows or blankets). I could hear students whispering while their eyes peered through the window slats, staring at us napping. They were annoying. They were curious about us, as we were curious about them. It was a cultural shock for me.

It was like the meeting of two different Filipino cultures—the privileged and the underprivileged. The only times mommy *allowed* us, siblings, to *mingle* with the underprivileged, was during our yearly Holy Week holidays to Madridejos or during our *Flores de Mayo* (May floral offerings to the Blessed Virgin Mary) summer sessions in San Nicholas church in Cebu.

I was probably in fifth grade when mommy told our yayas and our driver to take the girls to the *Flores de Mayo* summer sessions of San Nicholas Parish. Mommy was always too busy running her business that she always delegated her parental duties, which is perfectly normal for Filipino *negosyantes* (businessmen or women).

We were dressed in pink shiny satin gowns with *angel wings* (cut from cardboard and covered with white chicken feathers and strapped to our shoulders with a strong elastic string). Since we were the younger ones, we joined the other little girls walk slowly (with our palms together and the fingers straight, in praying position) from the church entrance toward the altar. The older girls walked behind us, as they held wooden poles carrying a letter of the words *Ave Maria*. The letters were formed from cut-out styrofoam covered with either pink or white *kalachuchi* flowers, whose lovely fragrance filled the church. Following the processional was no problem. The problem was understanding the Cebuano dialect. Our yayas had to translate everything to us.

Our first car was an an aqua blue Opel sedan with a white roof.

Our Opel was usually parked under the caimito tree, just in front of the front entrance door. Early 60s.

Then we had a beige window-less army jeep with all its sides open and a half door for the driver and the front-seat passenger. Much later, we had passenger jeepneys and other construction vehicles as my parents' businesses prospered.

Morning rush to school was frantic! Our *yayas* helped us get ready before 7:30 am, in time for Flag Ceremony. No one wanted to come *after* flag ceremony, which meant getting a late slip from the principal's office and mommy making an excuse letter for repeated tardiness. Mommy had no time for that. We relied on our yayas to wash, iron, and bring our clothes to our rooms, buy meat, chicken, fish, vegetables, and other staples from the wet market, and cook healthy meals for us. Although our yayas cleaned my room, mommy always reminded me to clean it and keep it tidy before I left for school, which I did.

Pick-ups were likewise interesting. At one time, Adam was picked up by a construction dump truck. It was the only vehicle available. Anyone could have seen Adam's face blush from embarrassment.

One Saturday morning, when one of our passenger jeepneys did not have a driver, daddy decided to pick up passengers. He tagged me along. I sat at the passenger seat behind daddy, who was on the driver's seat. I giggled every time a passenger rode the jeepney and paid his fare to daddy. The fare was P 0.25 for adults and free for kids. It was fun seeing daddy pretending to be a jeepney driver. With many poor Filipinos without private cars, commuting on public jeepneys was common. It was a fairly good source of income for my parents.

Around 1970, before Flint was born, we did not have a landline. While at STC, a wealthy classmate bragged that *they* had a telephone. Being the most articulate and the eldest daughter, I asked daddy and mommy to buy us one. Several weeks later we saw a classic, black rotary-dial phone, with a coil cord connecting the headset to the base of the phone, perched on a wooden ledge by the living room. It was the next most exciting gadget at home.

The most exciting appliance we had was the black and white television set. It had a twelve by fifteen inch screen inserted in a wooden casing with four wooden legs, perfectly situated in the middle of the room. It looked more like a furniture than an appliance. The usual shows were musicals like *The Amateur Hour* or *Tom Jones*, and a few horror movies. I don't remember watching a later night show with daddy and mommy since there was none. Sign off was about 7 pm.

On rare occasions when my parents came home late, watching TV was a social gathering for the yayas, children, and the many aunts and uncles living with us. As soon as the adults heard my parents coming in from the back door, my aunts and uncles would suddenly stand up and quickly go to their rooms. The yayas stood up too and became vigilant of mommy's *scolding*. The adults were always *scared of mommy's presence, as if mommy was going to bite them*. It was a hilarious scene!

While waiting for our pick-up after school, we stayed by the school music department, where we heard on-going music lessons. The music just mesmerized me. I wanted a piano too. A lovely, black, upright, *Mercedes* piano appeared in our living room after I asked my parents to buy us one. My sisters and I learned to play piano with the late Madame Ybod of STC's music department. Mommy had always wanted our family to be into music.

When Tres de Abril extension was not as traffic jammed as it is today, the unpaved dusty roads outside our back gate was ideal for playing. Full moon meant that the road was brightly lit and ideal to play *buwan-buwan* (moon-moon) with our neighbors. It was a game of tag around a water-drawn circle, with a line across. Players run along the water-lined path with the *it* catching anyone at arm's reach. As soon as we heard mommy call us, we scampered back home. She scolded us (in English) for leaving the premises of our house. It didn't stop us from having the next full moon adventure though.

Our house had lots of windows and no air conditioning. The only time we had an air-conditioned room was when I was 9, after Flint was born. Since he had allergies, his room had to be air-conditioned. A window-type air conditioner was installed between Flint's and my parents' rooms, making the room suitable for Flint— and the rest of us. Since the small room could only fit one single bed, for Ninfa (Flint's *yaya*), and Flint's crib, the rest of us slept on thin blankets, laid side-by-side, on the shiny waxed wooden floor. It didn't matter to us. All we needed was a good night's sleep.

Mommy was very particular about our caregivers. After six yayas, she found Ninfa. Ninfa said that mommy could not stand the previous yayas who just sat down and fan themselves after Flint went to bed. Ninfa was always doing something when our baby brother was asleep. She would either fix the clothes in the room, get Flint's next milk bottle ready or putter around the room, making sure that she did not leave the baby alone in the room.

While she started as Flint's personal nanny, she eventually became the household *Mayordoma* (governess). As mommy's distant cousin from Madridejos, Ninfa was loyal and obedient, she picked up English quickly, and —most important of all— she had the same *Commander-in-Chief* style mommy had. Ninfa got things done the way mommy wanted it. She freed mommy of most household responsibilities, giving mommy the chance to assist daddy with his myriad responsibilities.

Ninfa went with our family *everywhere*—to our Sunday outings in Pook, Talisay, our annual trips to Lawis, and even our summer trips to Manila and Baguio. While fufilling her nanny duties with Flint, she attended to the rest of us too. She became a vital part of our family, making a few relatives envious of her. They used to tease us that she became *the eldest member in our household, calling her Ninfa Salazar.*

She was so loyal and dedicated. No matter how many times mommy scolded her for doing simple mistakes, she continues to serve our household to this day. Before Ninfa's mom passed away, she told Ninfa to never leave our household, in gratitude for giving her a job at an early age. She was only about 20 years old when she started working for us.

Believing in education, mommy encouraged her to go to school. When Flint was a little older, and someone else could take care of him, mommy allowed Ninfa to finish her high school in Lawis. After she graduated high school and came back to Cebu, she was told to take a cosmetology course in a vocational school along Colon Street. She learned to cut hair and do nails. Surpisingly, mommy never asked her to do mommy's hair or nails. Mommy had them done at the posh *Maanyag Beauty Parlor* in uptown Cebu.

When SCSIT, our school, opened in 1983, she was encouraged to take an Elementary Education degree at the University of the Visayas since our school did not offer education at that time. After she graduated, she was given a job as a Teacher Assistant in the kindergarten classroom. She never passed the Teacher's Board exam even if she reviewed together with Cecile, who was reviewing for the physician licensure exam.

Og mo pasar ka basin diay mo pasar sad ko! [If you pass (the board exam) I might pass it too!] Ninfa wished loudly to Cecile as they sat side by side.

Nevertheless, Ninfa is still one of our favorites. We are forever grateful for Ninfa, and for all of daddy's and mommy's family, close friends, and neighbors, who sacrificed so much to help us during our early years. We have so many fond memories of them!

2 Corinthians 9:8 (ESV)

And God is able to make all grace abound to you, so that having all sufficiency in all things at all times, you may abound in every good work.

Five

La Obra Maestra

Eleven years after they tied the knot, daddy and mommy built their first home, had Salazar Construction Company, Inc. (SALCON), a Student's Bookstore, a franchise of a Mobil gas station, Salazar Engineering Review Center, Salazar boarding house, *six passenger jeepneys,* and mommy's rose business. Plus six kids. With their complementing management styles, mommy and daddy *had* to make things work!

They did not have wealthy parents, grandparents, siblings, or relatives to rely on. They depended on themselves. They had to risk all negative criticism coming from family, friends, employees, or neighbors.

My parents were dedicated and ambitious. They wanted to raise a family— different from the family they grew up with. A family having the comforts that life could bring, a family above and beyond the ordinary

Filipino household of that day. They had dreams and ambitions, something they had always wished for. Laziness and poverty were not an option. Daddy's wit and mommy's control of their businesses brought us to where we are today.

In 1964, when the CIT construction project was finishing, daddy and mommy decided to put up a *Student's Bookstore* across CIT. Their first bookstore employees included mommy's siblings (Toto, Titing, Totong, and Nene, her all-around business helper), her cousins (Danny, Done, and Toto *Simon)*, and daddy's brother, Ludy (as his all-around guy). Recycled materials from CIT's construction project combined with new materials were used to build the bookstore.

Employees of our Salazar Engineering Review Center, canteen, and bookstore. Behind them is the first building my parents constructed for these businesses. This is the current site of our family school, SCSIT. Natalio B. Bacalso Avenue, Cebu City, Philippines. Early 70s. (photo credit: Perla Aleria dela Torre)

Student's bookstore was constantly packed with customers. Their various supplies included books, much needed by their clientele, some of whom were my classmates.

When I was in 7th grade—the last STC batch in 1974, our literature teacher wanted our class to secure a book which was on limited stock in the bigger bookstores. I was very pleased to find a few copies of the book in *our* bookstore. As soon as I met my class the following week, I happily lent my books to my classmates, without even bothering to collect them back. Had mommy known that I *lent* books to my classmates, I could have gotten a big scolding.

Shortly after the bookstore opened, my parents franchised a Mobil gas station, the next block from the bookstore, toward J. M. Basa Street. The bookstore employees had to find time to help with our gas station. More employees were hired like Nonoy, another of mommy's cousin, and Roberto.

The gas station did not have a car wash or a convenient store. It just had a few gas pumps with attendants pumping gas to cars. It had a great location: across the second campus of CIT, close to *Taboan* public market and *Pasil* fish port, and the road leading to Colon Street, the main thoroughfare of downtown Cebu.

Mommy clearly recalled having gone on a free trip to Hong Kong, with daddy, as a reward for reaching the highest sales in a month, among other Mobil gas stations in Cebu. Although the gas station was doing well, there were safety issues which caused it to be closed down.

Meanwhile a Manila office, manned by Danny and Victor, needed to be opened. Manila, being the capital of the Philippines and the location of the seat of the government, was the strategic place to collect income for our ever-increasing government construction projects and a vital link to business networks.

While the sixties was the experimental era, the seventies and eighties were the investment times...when daddy and mommy made the empire grow and found their niche in society. While mommy was contemplating to leave her teaching job, one of her co-teachers pleaded for mommy to buy her property.

Ding (Naiding), palita akong yuta be, bisan data-datahan lang nimo, sa imong gusto. (Ding, please buy my property, even if you pay it by installment, at your terms.)

Ngano diay. (Why?)

Nasakit akong mama, wala koy ikabayad. (My mom is sick I have no money to pay.)

Mao ba? Wala man unta koy plano mopalit ug yuta karon, pero estoryahan sâ nako si Dodo. Og barato nâ, basin paliton namo para sa umaabot nga panahon. (Really? I have no plans of buying a lot nowadays, but I will talk it over with Dodo. If it's cheap, then we could possibly buy it for the future.).

Mommy bought the lot. Daddy called it Riverside since it's beside the Arrabal River. Incidentally, it's just several meters east of our first home in Labangon. Several years after my parents bought the lot, they finally decided to build some structures on it. Most of daddy's siblings were by then college students in Cebu.

It was time to relocate his parents, Lolo Nene and Lola Tonyay, from Sogod, Leyte, to Riverside, Labangon. At the center of the lot, daddy had his construction crew build a one-story concrete home for his parents. This was where Auntie Flor, Tiyo Ludy, Tiyo Beting, and Tiyo Mat also lived while they went to college. The Riverside lot looked like the city version of Sogod. It used to be spacious with only my grandparents' home at the center. That same lot is the present-day Executive Village, housing several apartments and houses for rent. Lolo and lola's original home still stands at the center of the village.

Tiyo Mat recently told me that Lolo Nene and Lola Tonyay paid P60,000 cash to mommy for the exclusive use of this home. Although daddy was not agreeable to it, the transaction was finalized.

Lolo used to make coconut shell charcoal from scratch. A hole, about eight by eight feet, and 6 feet deep was dug on the left side of the lot, just across lolo's house. Empty coconut shells were dried in the open pit until there was about two or three layers of fully-dried shells. Freshly-cut coconut palm leaves covered the top of the open pit when the dried shells were burned. Imagine the pungent and dark smoke coming from that pit! After several hours of burning the shells, out came the slightly burned palm leaves leaving the fully burned crisp coconut charcoal shells, called *uling*, perfect for cooking. Aside from making charcoal Lolo Nene raised chickens for home consumption. Like daddy, lolo kept himself always busy.

To cut lumber for our construction, daddy installed a bandsaw mill in Riverside. It was cheaper if he cut whole trees than to buy cut wood for his construction business. I would often get sawdust there for school craft projects. Sharing sawdust with classmates was a sure way of making friends.

Between Lolo Nene's and Lola Tonyay's house and the sawmill were lots of storage areas for scrap wood and metals and other construction materials which revealed daddy and mommy's knack for storing used materials for recycling. With a handful of skilled construction crew around, it was much cheaper to mix and match parts to repair broken equipment than buy new ones. Only the totally wrecked parts were sold as scrap material by the kilo.

Upon daddy's request, I visited my paternal grandparents on weekends during my high school days. I had lunch with them in their dining room, just adjacent to the living room. I was absolutely amazed to see that *all* windows and doors were decorated with lola's hand-crocheted curtains! She also hand-crocheted glass holders and coasters. She gave us, sisters, hand-made tatted veils to put on our heads while attending the Catholic Mass. Then lolo's style—being the physician that he was—was to use a 6-part compartmentalized plate, while the rest of us used regular porcelain plates.

By 1969, the first engineering review classes were held at Riverside. Daddy's first batch of reviewers were his working students. These students came from impoverished homes and worked entry-level jobs at daddy's construction firm, while finishing their college education. They could not afford to go to school without working at the same time, the same path daddy took. He was very kind to them since he knew the difficulties they had to go through.

Financial difficulties hindered the reviewers from reviewing for the board exam. At that time, the review classes were only held in Metro Manila. With daddy's review classes held in Cebu, it was more convenient and less costly for them. Their only hurdle was the actual exam in Manila. As soon as those working students passed the board exam, they were offered jobs in our construction projects. Daddy was very keen about actual hands-on training as the best way to learn and be hired quickly. What a privilege those students had!

By the early part of 1971, The Engineering Review Classes (renamed Salazar Engineering Review Center) was later relocated to South Expressway. The newly constructed one-storey building was built along Cebu South Expressway (*Highway*, as the locals call it). This was later renamed Rizal Avenue, and finally Natalio B. Bacalso Avenue that we know today.

The one-story building housed not just the Salazar Engineering Review Center but also the newly relocated bookstore, a canteen, the mimeographing room, and the management offices at the rear end of the building. Daddy's classmate, and favorite architect, Soy Suico and his wife, rented a unit at the front of the building.

Suico, as I called him, was shy and constantly smiling. He was a very talented architect. He created functional and elegant designs! He probably designed ninety percent of daddy and mommy's construction projects and custom-made furniture. Daddy said that he was not able to pass the Architecture board exam but he was nevertheless hired to be daddy's official architect.

To a nine-year-old, walking with daddy from our Tres de Abril home to the review center was a ten-minute adventure for me. I got to see our neighbor *kutsero* (a driver of his horse-drawn rig) tending to his horse and cleaning his *tartanilla* in their tiny makeshift stable. It was fun looking at the horse getting a mud bath in a the *kutsero*-made puddle. They cooled off after a hard day's work.

Mommy had always been adamant about us siblings observing and helping out in our businesses. That meant that we *had to go* to the office— including the bookstore and the canteen—during weekends, against our wishes. That practice eventually became useful to all of us, as we got older and started our own businesses. Learning the trade at a young age gave us an advantage.

There came a time when I started to enjoy going to the office. I stood behind the bookstore counter waiting for customers to buy an item or two. Since I could barely understand or speak Cebuano, I simply observed what our salesladies did. The best part about weekends in the office was the free meals and snacks from the canteen, located in the same room but across the bookstore area.

My office exposure also meant socializing with our employees, most of them were our relatives, neighbors, or family friends, who were *forced* to speak English to us siblings. We were not allowed to roam around the review center when there were classes. During lunch break, our canteen was full of reviewees and staff. Occasionally the reviewees bought their review handbooks —some of them were written by daddy and a few review instructors—and school supplies from our bookstore.

There was George, the jolly mimeographer, who was in charge of hand-cranking the mimeographing machine to make copies of review notes. He was also the life of the party, always happy and willing to do *any* job my parents would ask him to do.

There was also Loling, daddy's second cousin, with whom I enjoyed conversing. I talked to her about anything that came across my mind. She was smart, very open, and amiable. She had wit and humour, like daddy—and she was very good in English. I was quite comfortable with her.

Loling had a separate office to do documentation and legal paperwork. I liked staying beside her in her quiet office. It was a more relaxing place to stay compared to the noisy bookstore, canteen, review classes, George's mimeographing room, or the main office of daddy and mommy. Eventually, she married our legal counsel, like many of our employees meeting their soulmates through their employment with us.

Daddy's office. Labangon, Cebu City. 1970s.

Daddy and mommy's office is comparable to *Malacañang* (official residence of the President of the Philippines), with daddy as CEO (Chief Executive Officer) and mommy as CFO (Chief Financial Officer). There was lots of hustle and bustle there, from the *pandays* (manual laborers), asking daddy for cash for nails, or other construction supplies, to mommy's *suking agente* (favorite sales agents). These agents tried to sell to her the latest jewelry item or the best-priced property in the market. There were also engineers, foremen, draftsmen, other employees, or guests who came in any time of the weekday or Saturdays.

Lots and lots of employees became part of our businesses. The bookstore and gas station employees helped with the construction and review classes, too. Our first few office and construction employees were Tiyo Abring, Tiya Nening, Ruben Y., Joe, Mila, Uly, Perla, Alice, Belen, Jun S., Dionisio A., —and many, many more. Notable engineering review teachers were Engr. Besavilla and Engr. Dimagiba.

Daddy and mommy combined business and family holidays. One such holiday was when they were overseeing a big telecommunication building project in Quezon City—a major city within Metro Manila. We kids with our nannies had to tag along. Our two-month stay in a rented apartment in Quezon City was the longest summer holiday we ever had outside of Cebu.

I just turned 10 then. For the first time, we had exposure to the *real folks* of Manila. Our earlier Manila trips were booked in local hotels.

"Pakibili ng Dr. Pepper? (May I buy Dr. Pepper?... in Tagalog), " I heard Vicky, our nanny and eldest daughter of Leoning, one of daddy's trusted construction foremen, say to the young saleslady of the nearest *sari-sari* (corner store), to buy soft drinks for me.

Dr Pepper or *RC cola* weren't sold in Cebu. Tagalog (Philippine national language) was spoken in Metro Manila, and Cebuano Bisaya (one of major Philippine languages) was spoken in Cebu. While we learned Tagalog in elementary school, it was simply by rote memory.

Si Belen at si Ruben ay naglalaro ni Bagsik! (Belen and Ruben are playing with Bagsik—their dog). Belen and Ruben were the only main characters of our early elementary Tagalog books. It was pathetic!

Conversing with the Tagalogs was more than the *Belen and Ruben* line. It was exciting stuff... so delightful to hear and speak!

That summer all of us got chicken pox! Except for Cecile, who was always the last one to catch any illness. Poor Ninfa, Vicky and Nora had to take care of six children under eleven. As it turned out, house guests, Mr. and Mrs. Aranas had a grandson who caught chicken pox when they went to Baguio the week before.

As soon as we were all symptom free from the disease, it was our turn to go to Baguio—the summer capital of the Philippines. Baguio had an average temperature of ten degrees cooler than Cebu. Together with some Ifugao ladies in their native attire, we had a family picture at Mines View Park overlooking the mining town of Itogon, which used to be the gold and copper mines of the Benguet Corporation.

On another Manila trip, our family visited the Manila zoo where Ninfa carried the toddler Flint in her arms most of the time.

Our next adventure was *Shooting the Rapids* at Pagsanjan Falls in Laguna (still part of Metro Manila). My parents left the three younger kids at home with our nannies while bringing the three older ones to face this apparently treacherous *banca* (canoe) ride.

My parents and the kids sat on two tiny *bancas* managed by a skilled boatman for each *banca*. The men maneuvered the *bancas*, one after another, through narrow, rocky pathways of the swirling Pagsanjan River. Without life jackets, each one seated on a *banca* had to hold tightly to its sides. While the *bancas* swayed side to side, we swayed with it rhythmically! I felt the brisk cool water six inches from my fingertips. Daddy and mommy looked relieved when the hour-long water adventure was over. I was distraught after the ride. Had I been informed about how rocky it was, I could have declined.

In another family trip when I was in my early teens, with the Dakay family—our close family friends— this time, we were on an eleven-hour train ride on the way to Tiwi Hot Springs in Albay, southwest of Metro Manila. Unlike the novel bullet train in Tokyo, the outdated country train was packed, noisy, and dimly lit. Train tracks passed through large communities of various villages.

As it was nearing midnight...we heard...

Clank, thug, bubug, clink, thud....

"Children, put your hands over your head!

Hide under your chair!," Daddy shouted.

Then the train lights were turned off. Everyone was quiet.

Residents living along the railways were throwing stones at the passing train! But the train did not even slow down, it kept on moving. It must have been a usual incident since there was no announcement made by the train personnel over the P.A. system. *Would we ever make it to our destination?* was my anxious thought.

Philippine Airlines, the first Asian airline to cross the Pacific and the country's <u>flag carrier,</u> brought us to Manila one summer. I was probably in first grade when mommy told us and our *yayas* to get us ready for the holiday.

We are experiencing turbulence. Please fasten your seatbelt, the pilot hailed over the P.A. system.

Way back when full meals were served in the fifty-minute trip to Manila, the flight attendant hardly had time to sit when a strong gust of wind lifted our aircraft several meters up and suddenly dropped us several more meters down.

"Pray the Holy Mary, Abet," mommy worriedly told me, as I sat beside her in economy side of the plane.

Coffee, water, orange juice jiggled in their cups, dinner trays fell off the passenger trays, overhead luggage, hats, *pasalubong* (souvenir) items fell off the open racks above the passenger seats. I felt my stomach churn and my hair lifted off its roots. It was a terrifying experience! The three minutes of turbulence felt like three hours.

The worse family holiday was onboard a ship to Manila the summer of 1978. We were visiting Adam as a freshman in university.

Our family and the Dakay family *almost perished.*

It could have been just a *forty-hour* joyous holiday to Manila, sailing in between and around some of the 7,641 islands and islets of the Philippines, onboard one of the best and biggest among the inter-island ships. Sounds like the Titanic? But this ship wasn't hit by an iceberg, it was smashed by gusty winds, torrential rain, and massive waves!

A nice warm summer day in April turned into a horrifying nightmare. Just when the ship was about to cross the waters off Masbate Island— almost halfway of the trip—the sky suddenly turned dark, the wind blew hard, and the calm waves tossed wildly, as they rocked the boat frantically. Daddy told us to stay in our cabins with our heads down on our pillow, not looking out the porthole.

As I placed my head on my pillow, I heard the boat creaking as it rocked back and forth. The goodie-filled Tupperware container on the counter was also moving back and forth, with every sway of the boat. So did the curtains at the sides of the double decker cots. I took a curious glance at the porthole. All I saw was dark blue angry waves curling almost to the top of the porthole.

"Dahil may low pressure area papuntang Manila, dito muna tayo titigil sa dagat ng Masbate hanggang hihina ang hangin," (Since there is low pressure en route to Manila, we will have to stay here, off the waters of Masbate, until the winds die down) the ship captain announced calmly in Tagalog.

The ship's bow was supposed to kiss the Port of Manila in 12-15 hours, but that would have to happen much, much later. We were in the Visayan sea, across the island of Masbate, where the surrounding islands blocked those fierce winds from hitting the vessels.

We must have been in the eye of the storm. The waves became calm and quiet. Our ship was securely anchored. But passengers in the ship were getting restless and stinky. We stayed in that cove for eight days. From the porthole, I saw lots of big and small vessels anchored quietly on the waters, just like our ship. Food, water, and baby formula were running out. The ship's crew had to buy much need supplies from Masbate.

Surprisingly, our meals continued to be served by hospitable waiters (a privilege for first class passengers) in white long-sleeved polo shirts with matching black bow ties. Their *forced smiles* revealed clothes that had not been washed for eight days and shiny oily well-combed unwashed hair. None of us could afford to waste precious water for a bath. Potable water was consumed *strictly* for drinking, cooking or mixing baby formula.

Desperate to serve plated meals for first class passengers—most of whom were the elite of Cebu, the chef had to be creative. Since the ship's frozen food ran out, the kitchen crew *had* to use the passengers' frozen food cargo as food for *everyone* onboard. We were on survival mode.

I will always remember the 3-4 pieces of thinly cut pork fat, sautéed in oil, splashed with several cups of potable water with a dash of salt and pepper, as our soup for several days. Each spoonful of soup was savored. This was served with newly steamed rice.

It's hard to imagine what the third class passengers or the ship's crew had for their meals.

I often snoozed in a comfortable chair on the stairway landing. There were many people seated beside me or those going up and down the stairs. But I was unmindful of them. I was feeling cooped up in the stuffy cabin.

"Stay in your cabin!" Daddy reminded me.

I went to my cabin immediately. Daddy probably though how unsafe I was napping in a public place.

With compassion in his heart, Daddy gathered the first and second class adult passengers together and organized nightly prayers, an information brigade, and other vital endeavors, creating a bridge of communication with the passengers and the ship's crew. The group often met in the mess hall where lots of conversations took place. They had a name for their group.

Several weeks after this incident, daddy even invited this group for a grand reunion in our private Pook, Talisay beach resort.

On the eve of the ninth day...

"Medyo humina na ang hangin, bukas tatawid tayo papuntang Manila." (The wind has slowed down, We will cross the waters and head to Manila tomorrow). Yeeaaaaaay! Our nightly prayers were heard.

I hardly remember having the ship personnel distribute emergency life jackets—probably *because there wasn't enough for everyone* in the jampacked ship. There were men, women, children, and infants (and luggage) in the hallways, stairs, lobbies, and everywhere else I turned. During those times, ships were often overloaded with passengers, way beyond the limit set by the Coast Guard.

All my seventeen-year-old mind was thinking about was my sticky and oily hair which hadn't touch shampoo for awhile.

I docked my head once again on my pillow in the cabin that I shared with my siblings and Ninfa. I prayed the longest prayer ever then tried to sleep the night away. I was feeling like a baby rocked violently in a cradle in the herculean winds.

Day 9.

The ship tilted slightly to one side...not by the force of the wind, but from the *weight of the passengers who flocked to the east side* staring at the rainy Manila North Harbour...from a distance.

The heavy downpour looked like a beaded damask curtain separating the ship from the port. As the ship slowed down, I was delighted to see Adam standing astride, staying as close as possible to the edge of the port in an effort to have a glimpse of his family, nine days late. The ship's engine slowed down, until eventually the ship was docked safely...then *everyone* eagerly walked down the ramp to solid ground, unmindful of the rain around them.

"No more boat trips to Manila," mommy muttered in relief. Our next trips to Manila were by plane, and not with the whole family in one plane, but in two separate flights.

A relaxing Sunday with daddy and his friends at the front porch of our beach house. The group whom daddy organized in the nine-day 'adventure at sea' had a reunion here. Pook, Talisay. Mid 70s.

Watching the tennis match at our private beach house in Talisay. Mommy (with a sleeveless blue and yellow top) is standing behind the table at the right. The beach house at the background, behind the concrete wall, is owned by a Gullas family (another prominent family of Cebu). June 1976.

The tennis court of our private beach house in Pooc, Talisay, Cebu. Mid 70s.

To get away from it all my parents took short trips to other parts of the Philippines, U.S., and Europe.

Summer escapade to Baguio, the "Summer Capital of the Philippines". Early 70s.

(Left) My parents with Tiya Fannie and Tiya Tessie. Las Vegas. U.S.A. 1973.

(Above left) My parents needed Auntie Flor's help to repack their things before leaving Germany. Mommy's handwritten "Germany" on the picture.

(Above right) Final goodbye to Auntie Flor. Munich, Germany. 1976. (photo credit: Auntie Flor)

(Left) Meeting Tiya Marlene in Rome, Italy. August 1975.

(Below) Among the crowd of Vatican City. 1976.

They took a few tours of Europe and a visit to the pyramids of Egypt. 70s and 80s.

(Right) A handcarved china cabinet full of memorabilia of my parent's travels. (Below and the following page) Souvenir plates were mounted on wooden boards.

SALCON's multi-million construction projects afforded our family to take memorable trips—joyous or otherwise. It also generated more than enough income for my parents to purchase lots in an exclusive subdivision in Guadalupe, where we built *our second home*.

It took about two years to build our eight-bedroom ancestral home, excluding the maids' quarters and the garage structure. Meticulously designed by Suico, with a lot of input from daddy and mommy, majority of the home was built by daddy's construction crew.

The nipa hut at the far back was our playhouse. Daddy's construction crew built it exclusively for us. It was made of native materials. It had a 4-step wooden stairs leading to a tiny balcony. An actual kitchen sink was built inside the nipa hut. After we siblings got tired of playing in the playhouse nipa hut, it was given to Tito and his family. Tito (our uncle) was one of the trusted supervisors of our construction. Guadalupe, Cebu City. Early 70s.

Few subcontractors added the details. Each corner of the house was carefully designed to fit the space. Even the furniture were handcrafted and painted on-site. The furniture for the baby-blue boys' rooms were in matching hues and the furniture for the light pink girls' rooms also in matching colors.

While we still lived in Labangon, we visited our newly constructed home on some weekends. I watched daddy and mommy look carefully at several aspects of the building plans to make sure that each design was carefully carried out. I listened to Suico explain to my parents how each area of the architectural design would look like. I was fascinated to see that the drawn lines on paper would be replicated in actual space!

Whishhh, Suico would flip to page three of his structural drawings, as he verbally visualized how the floors would look like.

"Ang tanang sawug sa balay kay mogamit og white cement, nga naay mga bu-ak nga marble chips, aron mosinaw inig ka igo sa adlaw." (All the main floors of the house will be using white cement mixed with broken marble chips, so that it would sparkle when hit by sunlight.)

There were two full floors and two half floors. My eight-year-old mind wondered, *Was I going to live in Cinderella's castle?* Our second home was a *major construction project.*

There were still walls, ceilings, and posts to do. The roof of the front lobby was decked with an iron-fenced railing, turning it into a balcony—where our family stood every New Year's Eve.

Check the pattern on the floor of our formal anf informal dining rooms. April 2022.

We witnessed every fire cracker shot into space followed by kaboom or whooee-uueet-pop. As if that noise was not enough, we hit pots and pans with wooden ladles to make the loudest noise possible—to ward of evil spirits and welcome the New Year, as our *katigulangan* (ancestors) passed this on to us. When the sky turned dark and silent again, we went down to the formal dining room and ate our traditional Noche Buena (midnight dinner) of *puto, sikwate, manga, biko,* and *budbud.* Occasionally we had paella.

The balcony above the carport, as seen from the east-facing courtyard. June 2023.

Mommy's orchid collection. They had seen better days in the 70s and 80s. April 2022.

Every material used for every nook and cranny was carefully chosen for each specific function and design. It was amazingly beautiful and elegantly built! Most of all, it was huge, spacious, quiet, carefully crafted, and exciting to imagine! It was my parents' masterpiece!

"*Mura man nig mansion*," (This looks like a mansion!), Mrs. Martha Ceniza—daddy's second cousin—commented as she stared at the marbled walls and floors of the master bathroom with an ensuite tub. Relatives were often invited during the many banquets we had at the Guadalupe residence.

Some of our house warming guests with Mrs. Martha Ceniza at the rightmost. 1971.

During our house warming party in 1971, mommy hired a live band to play traditional music, called a caterer to serve dinner, and she requested a cook to roast a calf under the *tambis* tree. Jun-jun our caged "police" dog (German shepherd) barked incessantly at the cooks, servers, and guests who came close to him. Since his cage was under the *tambis* tree, he probably felt intruders all around him. Guests were seated in all corners of the house, the courtyard and the gardens. Close to a hundred men, women, and children were probably invited.

For extra security, my parents hired a residential security guard, although we already lived in a gated private subdivision with entrance security personnel. Ely Catamco watched our home, from six in the evening 'til 6 the following morning. His other job was to open the gate for any family member or guests to come in.

Within two decades of their marriage daddy and mommy owned not just a majestic mansion in Guadalupe, Cebu City, but several other prime properties in the Philippines. They ventured into banking when they opened the Rural bank of Madridejos in the 80s.

Daddy and mommy were always part of every program they participated in. Boracay, Aklan, Philippines. May 24-25, 2012

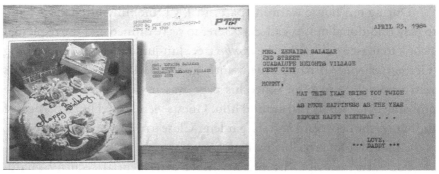

A birthday telegram to mommy from daddy while he was in Manila and mommy in Cebu.

Daddy and mommy's dreams, ambitions, dedication, perseverance, combined expertise—and most of all, their compassion to help the less privileged— brought them to become one of the successful members of their clans.

A self-made man. Engr. Doroteo Monte de ramos Salazar, taken during their 50th wedding anniversary. July 25, 2009, Cebu City. (photo credit: Lito Inso)

Mrs. Zenaida Figuracion Salazar. During their 50th wedding anniversary, July 25, 2009. Cebu City. (photo credit: Lito Inso)

Philippians 4:19 (ESV)

And my God will supply every need of yours according to his riches in glory in Christ Jesus.

Six

Surviving the Empty Nest

The USA trip was the last stop of my first—and last—thirty-day Europe tour with daddy and mommy. It was a reward for being the first among my siblings to finish university, and with honors at that. Our plane landed in Amsterdam, Netherlands. From there the Cebuano tour group—arranged by a very successful travel agency in Cebu City—boarded a bus which took us to about 25 countries in Europe, including Netherlands, United Kingdom, Belgium, France, Spain, Monaco, Italy, Greece, Switzerland, Liechtenstein—the world's 6th smallest country, Austria and Germany. The lady owner of the travel agency escorted us.

Fortunately Tiyo Eddie and Tiya Norma were with us—the same couple who went with us on that stone-throwing train incident en route to the Tiwi Hot Springs in Albay, in the 70s. About 45-50 Cebuanos spent a good month together, sleeping and dining in the same hotel. Majority of them were my parents' age.

The tour usually started with 7:00 am breakfast then 11:30-12:30 pm lunch, and 5:30-6:30 pm dinner. Since the tour was hectic and well-scheduled, each one had to be on time. Before the bus left every morning, the travel guide made sure that each tour member was present. We sat on the same seat all throughout the tour. I sat by the left window in the middle of the bus, where I saw everything so clearly through the big glass window, even through my Minolta camera lens.

Some full days were spent in the bus traveling from one city to another, like going through the Black Forest in Germany. In other days, travel times were just in a matter of hours. Shopping, sight-seeing, and taking pictures were always part of the schedule. Once in awhile, we talked to the locals or other tourists having similar itinerary as we had. We visited museums, gardens, fountains, churches, archaelogical ruins, forests, islands, plazas, tourist stalls, and much more.

Since each country had a different visa, our tall, brown-haired, non-smiling Dutch driver had to stop at every border to allow our Tourist Agent to collect our passports for inspection and stamping with the local Immigration Border Officials. Each country also used a different currency. So we had to exchange our US dollar for the local currency in every country we visited. After our month-long holiday, each of us had various currencies which served as part of our souvenirs.

Although I turned 21 a few months earlier, mommy gave me very little money. She had to save the money to buy bigger and more important things in Europe. I was still able to buy a few postcards and some knick-knacks, enough to please my simple soul.

The European food we had for meals was generally bland, lacking the Filipino soy sauce, vinegar, black pepper or *vetsin* (monosodium glutamate). After a few weeks of eating *bland* food, daddy got tired of it. He craved for the Chinese-Filipino taste. While in Paris, daddy made an effort to eat lunch in a Chinese restaurant. After lunch we went to the nearest street market where daddy bought red onions, soy sauce and vinegar. When we got back to our hotel, daddy used his *Swiss* pocket knife to cut the medium sized onion into small pieces. He dipped it into the soy sauce-vinegar fusion and ate them like dessert. He missed the Pinoy taste so badly. Mommy and I were amused at his concoction.

Still in Paris, our Cebuano group looked at the original—not imitation but the real, authentic stuff—shoes in a woodsy-smelling fashionable French shoe store.

"Are you speaking French?", the salesgirl asked us.

"Hehehe! No, we're speaking Bisaya!", we giggled.

After learning basic French and having lived ten years in Ottawa, where French is prevalent in many offices, I realize that the French language has lots of Spanish words—and so does the Cebuano dialect! Our French-sounding Cebuano gave us first class service from the lady store clerk.

Choosing goodies at a local store. Paris, France. May 8, 1982.

Mommy, a woman of fashion, bought an *Antique Vintage 8 Arms Cast Brass & Crystals Cherub Chandelier* from Paris, the Fashion Capital of the World. This original French vintage chandelier was shipped all the way from Paris to our Guadalupe home. As soon as the wooden crate arrived, our electrician, and his assistant, assembled each piece, one by one, making sure that each crystal hang perfectly under each bent-tip bulb.

The chandelier took center stage at the ceiling of the *only-for-special-guests* formal dining room in the mansion—a place reserved, and separated from the rest of the house, by an accordion-type floor-to-ceiling room divider.

"Asa si mommy ug si daddy? (Where are mommy and daddy?), I asked *'Nang* (short for *Manang*, a title for an older respected lady) Juaning, one of our caretakers at home.

"Tu-a sa gawas." (They are abroad.), our ever-smiling caretaker replied.

If I did not see my parents for many days, there was a high chance that they were in Manila or traveling abroad. They had the habit of *not* informing the kids where they were. *Was it to lessen the separation anxiety?* Yes teen-agers get separation anxiety too, especially when our weekly allowance of P100 (US $1.80) per week was running out. Although we did not communicate much, we longed for their presence especially during mealtimes.

Our caretakers always knew where they went, but they would not tell us, unless we asked. For long travels, they sent trusted office employees to look after us. 'Nang Juaning was one of them. Our caretakers always provided whatever we needed. We got used to their absence that we did not even care to ask anymore.

If the house was quiet—from the absence of mommy's daily loud reminders to our helpers—we knew that they were either gone for a business trip or a pleasure trip. This time, they travelled by themselves. Most of us were already in high school, with our own busy schedules.

Amsterdam was the last leg of the Europe tour. While I was seated in my KLM Economy seat, on our way to New York City, I imagined seeing the renowned NYC landscape, then I hummed Frank Sinatra's signature song...

> *Start spreading the news, I'm leaving today*
> *I want to be a part of it: New York, New York*
> *These vagabond shoes, are longing to stray*
> *Right through the very heart of it: New York, New York*

Daddy and mommy wanted me to *be* part of NYC too.

Although I pictured NYC as bright and exciting, we arrived at John F. Kennedy International Airport on a cloudy and gloomy afternoon, in mid-May 1982. Daddy hailed a *Yellow Cab* that took us to an equally dingy hotel in the middle of Manhattan. From my hotel room window, I clearly remember seeing a couple of chimneys billowing grey smoke, surrounded by the plain cemented walls of the adjacent tall buildings.

No, we did not have *Breakfast at Tiffany's*. We had hotdogs, coffee and hot chocolate at the nearest diner, which was a stone's throw from our hotel. Mommy decided to eat there, nothing fancy, just a place to chill out after a long, exhausting tour of most of Europe.

On our way there, we saw the iconic NYC smoke coming out of manholes from the streets. The NYC system history reveals that *this steam is part of the old water vapor heating and air conditioning system since 1882* (World Today News). My parents were as quiet as I was, fascinated yet a bit wary about walking along the cosmopolitan streets.

From New York we flew to Irvine, California, to the residence of Tiyo Boy and Tiya Fannie. After a few days, Daddy and Mommy went back to Cebu, to a partially empty nest. I spent the next six and a half years in *The Golden State*, taking more studies and raising a family.

Through the rest of the eighties and the nineties, our eight bedroom home was slowly vacated and converted into guest bedrooms. Most of us, and our kids, went either to America, *The Land of Milk and Honey*, Australia, *The Land Down Under*, or Japan, *The Land of the Rising Sun*.

"Mangabli kaha mo ug eskwelahan?" (Why don't you open a school?), a beloved relative once asked daddy and mommy.

"Bitaw noh, aron daghan matabangan nga mga pobre." (True, so that many poor people can be helped), was daddy's reply.

Opening a school was not a far cry from teaching reviewers to pass the board exams, or teaching fourth graders to pass their exams. Being teachers themselves, my parents knew the importance of education.

SIT (now known as SCSIT) Cebu City Main campus, Philippines. 2019.

Salcon Institute of Technology opened in 1983. Salcon was short for Salazar Construction Co, Inc., the construction firm daddy started. In 1986, the school was renamed Salazar Institute of Technology (SIT) then finally, Salazar Colleges of Science and Institute of Technology (SCSIT). "It opened the first and second year classes with 211 students taking the technical curriculum in the secondary department."

http://scsit.edu.ph/welcome-to-our-school/ Daddy wanted to have 211 as our first number of students since it was the number of our address in school, 211 Natalio Bacalso Avenue (formerly South Expressway).

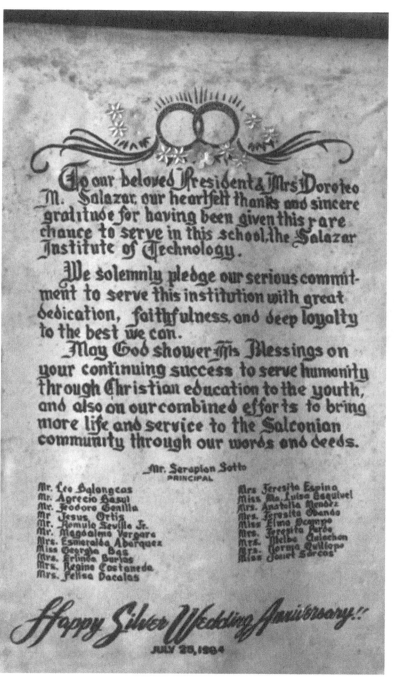

A gift from Dr. Sotto and the first staff of Salcon Institute
of Technology a year after the school opened.

By June 1996, Madridejos campus was opened. After daddy's first year of office as Madridejos Mayor, several parents requested to have a college opened since it was too expensive to send their children to college in Cebu.

SCSIT Madridejos campus. Cebu. September 18, 2023. (photo credit: SCSIT Madridejos-Supreme Student Government Facebook page)

They were the *cream of the crop* of selected public elementary schools of South Cebu. George spearheaded the school-to-school campaign in the first and second quarter of 1983.

Daddy gave back to society what hardships he experienced in college. These students were less privileged. Science and Technology was to be the emphasis of the curriculum, focusing on Mathematics as the major. With a successful Salazar Engineering Review Center to start with, and a high school and college kicking in, daddy had a vision to raise technocrats from his school.

In a couple of years, the Colleges of Business and Hospitality, Computer Studies (Information Technology), Criminology, Education, Engineering, Maritime, and Nursing, in both the Cebu City Main and the Madridejos campuses, were offered. Daddy and mommy were delighted to see so many young people finish college.

(Above) Red carpet entrance! Maritime students welcome the SCSIT Administration, SCSIT Cebu City Campus.

Criminology graduation. Madridejos campus. June 2023.

They were given the opportunity of their lifetime to have a quality well-rounded education, despite their parents' meager incomes.

College of Nursing's 20th Capping, Badging, Pinning, Investiture & Candlelighting Ceremony. Sacred Heart Center, Cebu City. June 6, 2023. (photo credit: AFS)

A parade of colors start the Founders' Week celebration. SCSIT Madridejos campus. February 2023. (photo credit: SCSIT Madridejos-Supreme Student Government Facebook page)

Founder's Day (presently called Founders' Week) was celebrated on February 4, on daddy's birthday. The whole school celebrated for a week leading to his birthday.

The SCSIT Drum and Bugle Corps (DBC) and banner bearers lead the Founders' Week parade along the major streets of the town. SCSIT Madridejos Campus, Cebu. February 5, 2023. (photo credit: SCSIT Madridejos-Supreme Student Government Facebook page)

(Above and below) The SIT DBC and marjorettes became champion in the interschool competition held at Plaza Independencia, Cebu City in 1992.

(Left) Their practice room was on the second floor of the building beside the clinic. After graduation the group continued to join, and win, in DBC competitions in several towns and cities. (photo credit: Gilbert Villarin)

(Left and middle) Mini Olympics opening parade joined by the faculty member and staff. SIT Cebu City Campus. 1992

(Bottom) Sports competition. February 1992.

(photo credit: Teresita 'Pompem' Antepuesto Gonzales, SIT High School Secretary, 1988-2009)

Various grade and year levels (preschool, elementary, and high school) and selected college students, teaching, non-teaching, and alumni competed in various sports competitions. The elementary and high school students had field demonstrations.

(Above) Students' field demonstrations. SCSIT Cebu City campus. February 2019.

(Left) Celebrating Founders' Week, with the theme 'Reflecting 40 Resilient Years'.

The jump ball officially start the basketball competition. SCSIT Madridejos campus. February 6, 2023. (photo credit: SCSIT Madridejos-Supreme Student Government Facebook page)

(Left) Miss SIT '87. High School Alumna 1988. (photo credit: P.R.L.M.)

The highlight of the week was Mr. and Ms SCSIT, which always culminated on February 4, daddy's birthday.

Faculty members, staff, or distinguished guests, are selected to award Ms. SIT. Rowena (second from the left) was Miss Teen Cebu City South, 1ˢᵗ runner up, and top 10 finalist in Ms. Teen Cebu City. She graduated high school from SIT in 1990. Miss SIT beauty pageant early 90s. (photo credit: Carol Basul Colin, Science Faculty member, 1983-2006)

Sports teams were created too. They competed interschool. Notable was the *Skyblazer* men's basketball team.

(Above) Daddy stands beside his winning team, the SIT Skyblazers. They were the high school champion during Cebu Amateur Athletic Association (CAAA), now known as the Cebu Schools Athletic Foundation Inc. (CESAFI). 1990.

(Right) Romarate holds the trophy together with Jun Mendoza, their coach. Recognizing Romarate's skills, daddy made him head coach of the school's high school varsity basketball team. He was able to train Jimwell Torion and Junthy Valenzuela to become stars of the Philippine Basketball Association (PBA).

(reference: The Freeman Banat News, September 10, 2023) (photo credit: Giovani 'Jojo' Romarate-Teves, SIT high school graduate 1991, Skyblazer team member 1987-1994, Skyblazer high school coach 1994-2020)

Being an exceptional point guard during his high school and college days, daddy's passion for basketball kept burning inside him. He made it a point to watch the PBA championships on weekend nights, whether he was in his bedroom in Cebu or in the living room of our Cubao, Quezon City residence.

When we spent our summer holidays in Cubao, daddy's eyes were always glued to the television, ears tuned to the commentator, carefully following all the points and the fouls going every which way. I totally enjoyed hearing the screeching of rubber shoes, referee whistle, or 'Time out!' screams of the coaches. It all sounded so exciting!

"There was a time during the Lakers championship he had me tape *all* the Lakers games and send them to Cebu for coaching purposes. There must have been over 40 VHS tapes shipped. The Lakers won the NBA championship for three consecutive years," Adam related daddy's request for him.

The Los Angeles' *Lakers* was definitely daddy's favorite basketball team, notably Magic Johnson—the 6' 9" point guard. The *Lakers* was his model for the *SIT Skyblazer* basketball team. Using the techniques of the *Lakers*, Daddy coached the first high school basketball team, when the school just opened. As soon as one of the players was good enough to be the coach, he relinquished his post. Jojo Romarate became the future coach of the *SIT Skyblazer*.

Whenever daddy was at the office, he watched his basketball team practice in the afternoons, on the very ground where he built his first home. Eventually the *SIT Skyblazers* made headlines, competing and winning several interschool competitions. Daddy volunteered our SCSIT students to do the statistics for most of the games. The team served as daddy's great advertising gimmick. More and more Cebuanos heard about SIT and decided to enrol.

Mommy, on the other hand, kept her business acumen going. Growing up with entrepreneurial parents, she learned to put every centavo to good use. She ran the school canteen, complete with an in-house bakery.

She went into real estate development, building affordable properties for rent in many parts of Cebu City, Lapu-lapu City, and in Metro Manila.

She convinced daddy to invest in more lots in other strategic locations in Cebu, including Bantayan Island. When pension houses were blossoming up in the city, mommy converted the front row of the apartment units of the Executive Village into *Zenaida's Pension*. It was good for awhile until mommy realized that converting it back into individual apartment units had higher returns.

I left the *nest* twice, in 1982 for California, USA and in 2010 for Ottawa, Canada. I was very fortunate to have my parents visit my family in both countries.

At mid-morning, on one snowy day in December 2012, just around Christmas season, when the frigid wind bashed my windshield, and medium-sized snow flakes were fluttering wildly around the car, I picked up daddy and mommy at the Ottawa Macdonald-Cartier International Airport. Winters in Ottawa usually last six months, starting from October all the way to April. December have mild winters, as compared to January or February.

"Abet this is *kuyaw* (scary)!", daddy commented while he sat uncomfortably beside me in my car.

"No 'Dy, it's just a small winter storm!" I assured daddy who was turning 77 in two months.

I was used to driving through winter storms in Ottawa, Ontario, two years prior to my parents' first time visit to Canada. Daddy—a little bit claustrophobic—felt *trapped* in the seven-seater *Mazda* van. He kept on moving around in his seat while looking out at the falling snowflakes. He had to bear the half-hour trip to our condo in Kanata, Ontario. Mommy sat quietly beside him.

"Tan-awon gyud nako unsa gyud ka bugnaw sa Canada."(I really want to see how cold it is in Canada). Daddy talked to Jun and Cecile at the front yard of our condo in *minus thirty five degrees centigrade—almost twice the temperature of the freezer.*

"Sure I can handle the snow!" Ottawa, Ontario, Canada. December 2012.

Jun, Cecile, and I were in our full winter gear—winter pants, jacket, tuque (warm knitted winter hat), neck warmer, socks, boots and gloves over our regular clothes—while daddy wore his pants, rain jacket, socks and house slippers. He got a bad sore throat the next day.

You don't play with Canadian winters! They hit you bad, especially if you are coming from a tropical country.

Daddy and mommy planned to stay a week with us in our home, but due to the extremely cold weather, mommy wanted to get rebooked on the first flight to the US to visit my other siblings.

"I want to know how to book my ticket to America."daddy talked to an airline personnel of Air Canada.

"I'm sorry I do not understand you. "the personnel replied.

"I do not understand you also, hahahahaha!" Daddy was amused.

The airline personnel did not get the joke. She looked perplexed. Daddy's over confidence confused the airline agent. All educated Filipinos speak English. But some of them speak it with a heavy accent (like daddy), quite incomprehensible to some Canadians.

Ottawa! Where winters can be -45 degrees centigrade. (Above left) With their granddaughter, in front of our condo. (Above right) Posing in front of the piled up snow. December 2012. (photo credit: Emily)

(Left) A joyful visit with other family members, Ester, Einon, and EJ. Ottawa, Ontario, Canada. January 2013

Paperworks followed him to Ottawa. Work was part of daddy's lifestyle. At our coffee table. December 2012.

I assisted daddy. We spent the next two days going back and forth to the airport, only to find out that the next flight out of Ottawa for the US would cost the same price as buying a new one. Mommy decided to stay until her regular flight took off, which was in three more days. She decided to *enjoy* their winter wonderland in freezing Canada

On the second day, a *balikbayan box* (a corrugated box used by overseas Filipinos) full of dried fish and other goodies from Cebu, was delivered to our doorstep. Daddy said that upon their arrival in Toronto, the airport authorities informed them the box will be sent directly to our Ottawa address.

It could have been inspected since it was an oversized luggage. My parents were delighted to see the goodies they had for us. We were likewise delighted! We got our favorite *danggit* and *nokos* (sun dried rabbitfish and squid).

The week was spent going to the Food Basics Supermarket, Walmart, Britannia Beach, and having dinners with extended family and friends. In the evening of the last day, we had a quick tour of downtown. Since it was Christmas time, there were lots of Christmas lights and décor everywhere.

A cherished family photo with daddy and mommy at Christmastime. Xi was always the Santa Claus, distributing gifts under the Christmas tree. This one is for his Papa Dodo. Ottawa, Ontario, Canada. December 2012.

It was beginning to look a lot like Christmas! Very festive and jolly, but lonely. There very few people on the streets to talk to.

Mommy needed help to get into her winter outfit. Every trip outside the house was a challenge for her. Simply stepping on snow with her winter boots was a bit scary for her. Her seventy-seven-year-old legs felt shaky walking on frozen ice. Someone had to hold her arm and walk beside her. Daddy, on the other hand, had no problem wearing his winter outfit or walking on snow. He finally realized that winter in Canada is no joke.

"They look like shoeboxes", daddy observed.

Having seen, and built, more complicated dwellings than those million dollar homes along the affluent area of Britannia Beach, his comments revealed his taste for well-designed residences. Daddy built roads, bridges, wet markets, schools, homes, substations, ports, commercial buildings, and other structures with more elaborate designs. Well, that's taking into account if the tropical climate in the Philippines allowed it. He and his partners also built an investment property in California. Ottawa homes have to deal with insulating the structures from the extreme cold and occasional rain, including having less and smaller windows and doors.

We siblings continued the alphabet by naming our sons and daughters with the letter corresponding to the one who was born next. Now they have almost twenty grandkids.

When mommy celebrated her 75th Diamond Birthday in 2010—and daddy turned 74— she had her first great granddaughter. Her name starts with an 'A'. The six great grandchildren came within nine years, from the first one.

"Papa and mama repeatedly stressed the importance of valuing food and minimizing waste. We had to finish every grain of rice during mealtimes.

We were exposed to simple life in rural areas while visiting our properties in Sante Fe and Madridejos in Bantayan island, Naga and Santa Rosa island in Cebu.

They hid negative news from us grandkids.

Every Saturday morning papa drove all of his grandkids on a trip to the nearby gas station, *skina* (corner) Banawa. He bought almost anything we asked: donuts, fresh milk, gum. Mama may not have known this.

Every encounter with salesgirls and salesmen was advertising for SIT. Papa would ask if they finished studying and go from there.

Papa and Mama stressed the importance of prayer and faith.

They made it known that the lifestyle we were living was very fortunate and done by wealthy people. We should be thankful for it. It would not last forever so we have to study hard and rely on own own success."

Chris, their second grandchild. Cerritos, Southern California, USA. August 30, 2023

When Anthony (the oldest of the grandkids) was wed to Sayo (a Japanese national), my parents, Christopher (his younger brother), and I came to their wedding in Chiba City, Japan, a few days before August 9, 2011. We had a site seeing tour of Tokyo before the wedding date. We took a forty-minute bullet train ride to Tokyo where we took walks through parks and explored the downtown core.

"When we were younger, I went with your mama to many places like Europe, North and South America, and Australia.

But it's only in Japan where we see the Japanese people who are perfectionists", daddy commented while walking through a downtown garden.

(Above) My parents lag behind my sons while walking through the gardens of the Meiji Jingu Shrine. (Below) I carried mommy's stuff so that she was comfortable. Shibuya, Tokyo, Japan. August 8, 2011.

Daddy was very impressed to see everything in Japan so perfect, from the manicured lawns to those skillfully-made pastries. My parents loved visiting other cultures and experience life in foreign countries. Unlike their earlier Europe trip with me, when they were still in their late forties, this first and last Japan trip was exhausting for them. They kept on stopping and sitting on benches around the tourist attractions, where they stretched their legs and caught their breath.

While we window shopped and looked at the throng of people walking the downtown streets, we were getting hungry. We saw a fancy restaurant along the main road and a small eatery under the railway bridge near the Shibuya station. Mommy asked daddy to convert into Philippine pesos the prices of a bowl of yakisoba noodles from those two places. She realized that she would be spending much less if we ate at the small eatery, for the same type of noodles. She decided to have meals in the small eatery.

Having lunch in an eatery for the common folks under the railway bridge near the Shibuya train station. Tokyo, Japan. August 8. 2011.

Anthony and Sayo's wedding. Honda chapel of Oyumino Christ
Church, Chiba City, Japan. August 9, 2011.

Whenever we had family gatherings, mommy was always expected to pay for our meals, as the matriarch of the family.

Anthony smiled seeing his wealthy grandparents having a quick meal in a place normally for the the lower income customers.

The night before the wedding, there was a formal gathering of Anthony's and Sayo's families. Daddy, mommy, Chris, and myself represented our family, while Sayo's parents and her siblings represented their family. While there were emcees to translate the general flow of the program from Japanese to English, and vice versa, the small table conversations between daddy and Sayo's dad was done in two languages.

"Sayo's daddy was telling stories in Japanese and I was talking to him in English. We did not understand each other so we just laughed!"

Daddy had a habit of laughing at uncomfortable situations he got into. Totally humorous! Mommy was the total opposite. She kept her silence, probably from embarrassment.

A toast to health, happiness and prosperity! Suisu-tei restaurant at Seimei no Mori (now called Resol no Mori), Nagaramachi, Chouseigun, Chiba, Japan. August 8, 2011.

Let's rewind back to the day when Anthony spent his first year in Los Angeles, California in 1986.

It was very memorable to *Papa Dodo* and *Mama Naiding* (Anthony's names for them). We spent a few months together in our Cerritos home. Since I was a stay-at-home mom, I spent all those days with them.

They kept their early morning routine of getting up before eight in the morning, having coffee with bread and later some light meals with rice, then reading the *LA Times.*

(Above left) Long Beach, California, USA. Grandparents with their first grandson, Anthony. February 28, 1987.

(Above right) At our Cerritos home. March, 1987.

(Left) Spending time with more family members. Culver City, Southern California. September 2, 1987.

If they were in Cebu they would have read the *Freeman* or *Sunstar*, with the radio blasting from the kitchen counter behind then, about the latest local political news. Once in awhile daddy would call the radio station announcer to comment on an issue especially when his name was mentioned. He was always abreast about the goings-on in town. LA was different. They were just content with a quiet breakfast.

Once a week, daddy cooked his favorite *pochero* (Filipino beef shank stew)—overflowing with his favorite *shiitaki* mushrooms, squash, cauliflower, potatoes, green onions, and *saba* banana. It was a sumptuous meal for all of us. Daddy cooked Filipino food better than mommy and me.

"Gusto makig-istorya unta si Tomas (Tommy Osmeña) *nimo bahin sa sitwasyon sa Cebu."* (Tomas wanted to talk to you about the situation in Cebu.) Tiyo Boy excitingly informed daddy.

"Ngano man?" (Why?)

"Ako siya gi ingnan nga dako kang tao sa Sugbo. Gusto lang siya makahibawo sa situation, kay mo lansar siyag politika didto. " (I told him that you are an influential person in Cebu—*Sugbo* is the ancient name for Cebu City. He just wants to know the situation since he is running for public office there.)

"Anhi lang 'ta sa balay ni Beth." (Let's have dinner here in Beth's house.) Daddy eagerly invited Tommy over even without informing me beforehand.

I gasped in excitement! Daddy just invited a member of an influential poltical family to our home. What an honor!

Having lived in the US for many years, Tommy was curious about the political climate in Cebu City. Since his family was always politically inclined, he was bound to join politics, sooner or later. Tiyo Boy and Tommy had been in the same Filipino circle for many years. Since daddy had amazing achievements, over and above the achievements of many of their contemporaries, Tiyo Boy thought that Tommy should be able to gather insights from him.

I cooked *pochero* for them. When he came for dinner, the trio had a long serious chat, after the meal. I noticed that daddy did most of the talking, while Tommy and Tiyo Boy, with both hands on the table and leaning forward towards daddy, listened intently. They tried not to miss a word that was said. I stood from a distance pretending to do my kitchen chores. The following year Tommy Osmeña became Cebu City mayor.

'Twas in the summer of 2016 when daddy and mommy crossed the big ocean again to visit their growing family in America. They flew from coast to coast to accommodate family celebrations and schedules. We visited iconic sites then we drove to Florida to enjoy the sun and the beach.

"Cecile, do you have a laptop?" Daddy wanted to catch up with work even while he was on holiday.

Working was daddy's leisure. He enjoyed it! He was constantly thinking about how to make a change, how to document changes, and how to implement them. He would rather do things himself, instead of delegating it to a secretary, which he never had, and which mommy would *never* allow him to have.

By this time, his focus was on the school. Although he turned 80 that year, he was still active in the daily operations of the school. Daddy always found ways to make things work.

He changed the name from Salazar Institute of Technology to Salazar **Colleges of Science** and Institute of Technology so that he could offer nursing. Our school got its very first board topnotcher, Ranking 10 in the November 2021 Nursing Board Exam.

> *Marie Hanz Therese Espina of the Salazar College of Science and Institute of Technology – Cebu City shows the checks she received for making it to the Top 10 of the November 2021 Nurse Licensure Examination.*
> http://scsit.edu.ph/maria-hanz-espina-top-10-board-top notcher/

Every minute of their American holiday was not wasted. They enjoyed the presence of their kids, grandkids and great grandkids.

Precious time spent with daddy's great-granddaughter, Tali. Guadalupe, Cebu City. December 2016. (photo credit: Chris Odtohan)

Daddy's habit was to place the youngest family member on his lap and make them giggle. Mommy enjoyed chatting with them, asking questions like:

"How old are you now?"

"What grade are you?".

When they were home in Cebu, they called family from across the seas, sometimes ringing in the middle of the night, unmindful of the difference in time zones. Daddy dialed the number, mommy talked.

"What time is it?"

"When are you coming home?"

If we could get up in the wee hours of the morning we had to answer her questions and make up answers, or she wouldn't stop asking until she was satisfied.

"Golden ang akong mga apo!" (My grandchildren are golden!") Mommy told Nang Juaning one time.

Proverbs 17:6 (ESV)

Grandchildren are the crown of the aged, and the glory of children is their fathers.

Seven

The Prize of Giving Back

Had we left the day after the May 10, 2004 mayoral elections in Madridejos, Cebu, we could have witnessed horror!

It was just after six in the evening. Daddy and mommy were resting in their upstairs bedroom from a long day, awaiting the results of the elections. They hadn't had dinner yet, nor did the rest of the household.

BANGG! BANGG!

Gun shots were fired from outside the gate, towards the sky, and above the house. Ritz (mommy's nephew), who was in the courtyard, talking with daddy's election staff about the possible election results, ran quickly inside the house. He was informed by daddy's bodyguards that there was plan for the political rival's goons to come in the house and slay him.

"Pag-nga ang mga suga ug ang planka! Dali!" (Turn off the lights and the switches of the circuit breaker box! Fast!) Ritz shouted to the staff.

In total darkness, Ritz ran quickly up the stairs toward my parent's room. Ninfa followed upstairs, holding a lit candle on her right hand. Hearing commotion in the hallway, Daddy—with his magnum 25 revolver in his hand—opened their bedroom door. Mommy was pale and hysterical! Daddy was trying to be calm.

"*Dali! Manaog 'ta! Adto mo tago sa storage room sa ilawom sa hagdanan!*" (Quick! Let's go downstairs! Both of you hide in the storage room under the stair landing!), Ritz whispered.

Without hesitation, my parents crawled quickly down the wooden stairway, with Ritz and Ninfa crawling beside them. They squeezed themselves through the meter-wide opening of the musty pots and pans built-in storage. Just when they were about to go inside...

"*Time pa, nabilin ang akong bag sa ta-as! Kuhaon nato!*" (Wait a minute, I left my bag upstairs! Let's get it!), mommy worriedly whispered. Daddy sighed.

"*Sige Tiya, kamang nasad 'ta sa taas,*" (Ok auntie, let's crawl up the stairs again.). Ritz hesitantly accompanied her upstairs again.

As soon as mommy and Ritz came down, daddy turned over his magnum 25 revolver to Ritz, in case he needed it for extra protection.

With hardly any legroom, they could only crouch on the floor and lean against the pots and pans, other odds and ends, amongst dust and cobwebs. It was a life-and-death experience they *never* expected to happen. It felt like forever!

Shortly after, Ritz called his dad (mommy's younger brother, my Tiyo Toto), PCpt Pedrito Figuracion, Sta. Fe's Chief of Police, and asked to be rescued. Tiyo Toto wasted no time to call PCol Y. and inform him of the crucial situation. He also instructed daddy's bodyguards not to fire their guns, while waiting for the rescue team. Ritz informed Eduardo (in Cebu) about the situation.

The residence was lit only by candles and gas lamps. No one was allowed to come inside the residence, not even the staff who remained in the courtyard. *It was too dark and too risky to let anyone else come in*, Ritz thought.

While there was deep darkness and silence inside the residence, there was chaos outside the gate! The people in the plaza, across my parent's house, scampered for safety! The military men, who had been stationed in this town a few days before election, and daddy's bodyguards, were the only ones left in the plaza. The gunman, who fired the shot earlier, had left the scene.

All the security men were on RED ALERT!

A body guard was posted inside the house. Others positioned themselves against the people entrance of the solid metal gate and by the *atabay* (water well), in front of the verandah, below my parents' second floor bedroom. The rest of them were stationed outside the gate.

Daddy instructed his security personnel not to use the weapons, unless needed. Then it happened. When one of his rival's goons attempted to open the people entrance of the gate, Balo, one of daddy's senior bodyguards, shot the back of his hand— to forewarn others. No one else tried to come in. They left quickly.

Very soon after, PCol Y. and his men, arrived at the gate. Since no one of daddy's staff knew him, Ritz requested the officer to remove his shirt, in the effort of finding any weapon in his person. After none were found, he was allowed to come inside, by himself. The rest of his men waited outside the gate.

As soon as daddy's staff confirmed that it was indeed PCol Y., they started to appraise him of what transpired. Lots of assessment made, lots of questions asked…*everyone* anxiously thinking about an escape plan.

Soon after, Tiyo Toto arrived to assess the situation thoroughly.

In the meantime, Ritz called Eduardo again to inform Flint not to come to the residence. Unfortunately, Flint was already driving toward the residence (from our beach house in Tarong), when bullets were fired *at* him! He quickly parked his car in a safe place between houses, along the road. He spent the night in one of those homes (one of daddy's allies).

In the early hours the following morning, when the streets were quiet, he drove to the residence to check on daddy and mommy…and everyone else.

After a series of phone calls and negotiations, Eduardo was finally able to charter a helicopter to pick my parents up from the Bantayan airport (half an hour away). Ninfa quickly packed their belongings. The night scene around the residence was eerily quiet. But inside, more planning and coordination happened in whispers… among various members of the rescuing party.

Mommy shared her cookies with everyone in the house. *That was their dinner.*

At around nine in the morning the following day, the body guards and house helpers loaded my parent's luggage in the car. After a simple and quick breakfast, Daddy and mommy were in the car with tinted windows. Our Madridejos-based family driver whisked them to the Bantayan airport—a small community airstrip, the only airport on the island. They boarded a chartered helicopter heading toward the Mactan-Benito Ebuen Air Base in Cebu.

Half an hour later, they arrived safely in the military airbase. Before noon, they reached their Guadalupe residence totally exhausted, where they were welcomed by a tableful of breakfast treats prepared by their helpers.

Knowing about the strafing incident through a text message, I visited them around noon. I was surprised to see no less than thirty people settling uncomfortably on the front and side lawns. Everyone— including daddy and mommy—looked tired and defeated. Fear still gripped them!

Daddy's mayoral rival was suspected of trying to get rid of him. The Freeman News (as quoted by The Philippine Star) released a report on May 13, 2004, that since Madridejos had been *placed under Comelec control on Election Day itself,* several police and army had been stationed there.

It was noted that gunshots were fired in the late afternoon of election day. It was further noted that there was a previous altercation between the Madridejos Chief of Police (rumoured to have close ties to daddy's mayoral rival) and a member of the army unit detailed to that town.

In another news article on May 14, 2004, daddy's name appeared as the *accused mastermind* of the gunshots fired on election day. Daddy, of course, denied these allegations.

Nothing was written about the strafing incident at his residence.

Although his opponent won, was the strafing incident necessary? Did daddy's opponent win by a slim margin? Was the election rigged? Since the incident happened just when the winner was about to be declared, did the rival make it evident that she was in control? How could the security officers of the town not respond to the gun shots, when the police precinct was just a block away? What if my parents remained in their Madridejos residence that night, could there have been bloodshed?

Where did they go wrong? Will they be safe now at their Guadalupe residence, six hours away? What was there to do?

As I *blessed* the hands of daddy and mommy, I saw the exhaustion and weary looks on their faces. They looked very unsettled. *This is our second life*, they must have thought. They were more comfortable narrating to their staff than to their children. I refused to understand the complexity of the situation. I was glad that they were safe. *Or were they?*

They held office from their home, too fearful about leaving. They could not focus on their work. Daddy spent a lot of time with his personal body guards and with the concerned staff recalling, recollecting, and analyzing the horrifying incident—trying to find loopholes in their plans, finding someone to blame, finding another way out of this troubling mind game.

Instead of vengeance, they sought escape. My parents gathered their documents and decided to take a break.

In two weeks, they left for the US where they stayed for several months in Adam's home. There they were able to rest and recover. They wanted to ally their anger, frustration, fear, and helplessness. Where were they heading? Is it really worth fighting for, the people of Madridejos? Should they really risk their life and finances knowing that politics is always a dirty and expensive game?

For the safety of the students, teachers, and personnel after the strafing incident, daddy decided to close the Madridejos campus of our school for a few years.

Our family is grateful to Ritz (left) and his dad, PCpt Pedrito Figuracion "Tiyo Toto" (right), for their efforts to ensure the safety of my parents during the strafing incident. (photo credit: Ritz Figuracion)

"Was daddy Mayor of Madridejos before?", I checked mommy's memory when I visited her around her 87th birthday on April 23, 2022.

"Yes, but not anymore. It's was very *gasto (expensive)*, speaking in our usual Salazar English—a combination of English and Cebuano.

With poverty rampant in the Philippines, especially in the smaller islands and countryside, those running for politics are expected to spend *a lot* for their constituents.

While daddy lost the mayoral elections in 2004, he *was* already Madridejos Mayor.

Progress was focused in Bantayan town proper. It took anywhere from half an hour to forty-five minutes ride to Bantayan either by *tricycle*—a sidecar attached to a motorcycle which serves as a common transport throughout the Philippines— or a bus (with only two schedules a day). Private vehicles were either used by few local businessmen or the municipal employees. It was in the bigger town of Bantayan that the *Lawisanons* would be able to visit a medical specialist, purchase gasoline, ice blocks, and other necessities; meet their banking needs or get a college education.

Instead of moving forward, the sleepy town seemed like going backwards. Being known as the *Little Alaska of the Philippines* (Wikipedia), it had the first sardine canning factory in the Philippines. It was unfortunately bombed—*suspected as done by the Japanese*—during the Second World War. Without electricity, a local bank, or safe water supply, Madridejos did not prosper as much as it should have.

"We had light before the war, but now no more," Lolo Usting narrated in broken English, as he pumped the *petromax* in his Madridejos residence.

From the 50s to the 70s gas lamps, candles or flashlights lit the evenings of the town. Since we did not have a car there, we used to walk to our destination, covering our noses with handkerchiefs as we walked on dry, dusty roads. Through the years, daddy understood the plight of the *Lawisanons*.

My parents used to just go with the flow of the town activities until the mid 90s, when the municipality of Madridejos got so impoverished that the local town officials had to *seek public donations to pay for the town's utilities*. Knowing that daddy was married to a *Lawisanon*, the influential residents of the town sought his help. They were banking on his significant achievements in Cebu as well as other parts of the Philippines.

Out of his deep compassion for the *Lawisanons* and his love for mommy, her siblings, and extended family members, daddy conceded to run for public office. With mommy's visibility as Acting Mayor in the late 80s, the presence of their residential home in the Poblacion—the town centre—and the generations of significant business activities in the town, daddy thought that this track record could possibly win the hearts, and votes, of the townfolks.

With the help of the volunteer spirit of the local youth, family members, and businessmen and women, daddy was given the chance to improve Madridejos.

> "...the mayor brought with him his rich experience as an entrepreneur, an educator, and a civil engineer. Unlike his predecessor, he was ambitious, wanting more for Madridejos than being a poor cousin to the neighboring town of Bantayan."
>
> *Reference: Sino Cruz, I. R. (1996, August-September). The Miracle that is Madridejos.* The Freeman Magazine, *p. 9.*

They brought back Madridejos to be a vibrant and prosperous town. With the great help of the local officials, he was able to gain the trust of the local town folks to join, and be active, in the town's Chief Executive plans and visions.

This combined community effort elevated Madridejos from 5th class to 4th class municipality in the Province of Cebu.

"DOROTEO M. SALAZAR -

Mayor. July 1, 1995 –" is printed in bold under daddy's black-andwhite picture—a vibrant-looking, dark-haired, middle-aged gentleman, wearing a white native *barong tagalog* (a national Filipino formal shirt), bearing a promising smile. After 1995 – is a blank space, showing marks of being tampered. He was mayor of Madridejos for two consecutive terms, 1995-1998 and 1998-2001. In 2007-2010, he won as Vice-Mayor of Madridejos.

A few pictures away from daddy's picture was mommy's. Their pictures still hang among the uniformly-framed pictures of Madridejos' past mayors, on one of the walls of the town's Municipal Hall.

Madridejos past mayors.

Worth noting is the hosting of the 1996 Cebu Provincial Meet in Madridejos. It was the first time that Bantayan island hosted such event. Daddy was able to build an Olympic-sized swimming pool and a standard track and field oval using funds from his own pocket. Through sports development, the *Lawisanons* had a taste of excellence in sports, successfully competing with other athletes in the Province of Cebu, and in the whole Philippines, in the *Palarong Pambansa* (National Games) in General Santos City and the Cebu Athletic League on July 14, 1996.

On opening day of the 1996 Cebu Provincial Meet, daddy ran with the torch bearer in the olympic size track and field oval which he had built. It is located in the Madridejos Provincial High School (now known as Madridejos National High School). Madridejos, Cebu.

The track and field oval still exists today. September 11, 2023 (photo credit: Reydito Cena)

A few years after hosting the provincial meet, Madridejos was awarded the "Galing Pook" (Best Community) Award.

This award was given to a local government for enabling the youth to participate and excel through its Sports Development Program, as well as encouraging the rest of the community to engage in livelihood activities, the conservation and protection of their environment. These were all through the efforts of daddy as Madridejos Mayor, supported by his local officials.

Awarding of the "Galing Pook" award. Malacañang Palace, Manila. January 20, 1999.

Receiving the "Galing Pook award" for having one of the cleanest and greenest Local Government Unit in the Philippines. Malacañang Palace, Manila. January 20, 1999.

My parents' involvement with the community gave them more opportunities to meet and mingle with politicians and celebrities.

A pose after dinner with the former Vice President Joseph "Erap" Estrada (center seated), the Philippine cinema's "Superstar" Nora Aunor (right side seated), and the former Congressman Benhur Salimbangon (left side seated). They visited Madridejos for many political reasons. Joseph Estrada "became the 13th president of the Philippines (1998-2001)". Nora Aunor is a "Filipino actress, recording artist, and film producer". Benhur Salimbangon "served as Board Member of the Fourth District of Cebu (1992-1998)" and "elected to the House of Representatives of the Philippines in 2007". (Wikipedia). Madridejos, Cebu. September 25, 1997.

A rare visit of national celebrities to Madridejos.

When daddy won his second term as Madridejos Mayor (1998-2001), mommy became his Vice Mayor. Both of them had the chance to visit the former President Fidel V. Ramos, the 12th president of the Philippines (1992-1998). Malacañang Palace, Manila. 1998.

Richard Gomez, movie actor and politician, visited the town to launch Richard's MAD "Mamamayan Ayaw sa Druga" project, a campaign against the use of illegal drugs. Richard "is a Filipino actor, television presenter and director, politician, and épée fencer. He has been serving as the Representative of Leyte's 4th district since 2022, and was mayor of Ormoc, Leyte from 2016 to 2022." (Wikipedia) Between Richard and daddy is Rev. Fr. Nilo Igloria, parish priest of the Immaculate Conception Parish then. Madridejos, Cebu. 1997.

Campaigning for the former President Benigno "Noynoy" Aquino III, 15th president of the Philippines (2010-2016), son of the assasinated politician Benigno Aquino Jr. and the 11th president Corazon Aquino (1986-1992). Noynoy "served as a member of the House of Representatives and Senate" (1998-2010) (Wikipedia). November 18, 2009.

Madridejos is mommy's birth town, and daddy's adopted hometown. He met mommy's relatives in many occasions.

Family gathering. Madridejos, Cebu. May 2017.

(Above left) *Fr. Randy Figuracion, SDB, described his fondness of my parents during the 2014 Figuracion Clan annual reunion, Madridejos, Cebu. (photo credit: F.M.A.F)* (Above right) The former Madridejos Mayor enjoys his favorite *coffee and "pan de sal" (Filipino breakfast bun). Salazar Residence front porch, Madridejos, Cebu. 2016.*

Being a Madridejos native, Mommy had her stint in politics. As an offshoot of some election-related controversies, mommy served in the

ZENAIDA F. SALAZAR - Acting Mayor
Nov. 11, 1987 - Feb. 1, 1988

Mayor's office short of three months. Upon the prompting of family and friends, she ran for office in 2001. Her political rival *allegedly rigged the election* and won as Madridejos Mayor. Mommy's rival for the 2001 elections was the same rival of daddy in the 2004 elections.

"ZENAIDA F. SALAZAR – Acting Mayor. Nov. 11, 1987 – Feb. 1, 1988" was written under her picture—a well-painted face with a confident smile. She wore a *kimona* (a traditional Philippine costume for women) with a floral scarf on her left shoulder. Her hair, put up in a bun, was adorned with flowers on the right side of the bun. She wore hanging double-beaded earrings and a white beaded necklace.

When daddy won his second term as Madridejos Mayor in 1998-2001, mommy was his vice mayor.

One of mommy's achievements was the construction of a welcome arch to the town of Madridejos. It was strategically situated on the boundary between the towns of Bantayan and Madridejos. Another project was to line the major street with multi-colored bougainvillea flowers, from the welcome arch to the major hub of the town. It was patterned after streets in Europe.

To awaken the historical past of the town, mommy cleaned and beautified Kota Park, *Presidio de Lawis* in Spanish. It used to be a Spanish era fortification which was built around 1628-1630. It served as a watch tower of the Lawisanons to protect themselves from the Moro pirate during the Spanish era (Wikipedia). Through the years, Kota Park sadly became a public cemetery.

Mommy had the Immaculate Conception Church renovated and improved the plaza just across the church. She had pine trees planted as well as had the fourteen stations of the cross built around the Poblacion Plaza.

One of the fourteen stations of the cross built during mommy's term as OIC Mayor of Madridejos. August 17, 2023. (photo credit: B. ^B.)

Her faith and involvement with the church made her and daddy the 2001 "Hermana and Hermano Mayores" for the Feast of Senior Sto. Niño for the Basilica Minore del Sto. Niño de Cebu in January 2001.

Hermana and Hermano Mayores" for the Feast of Senior Sto. Niño in 2001.

(Above) Even before daddy started his political career, his political connections brought him and mommy to the White House. They were invited to attend the inaguration of George H. W. Bush "as the 41st president of the United States" and Dan Quale as vice president. It was held at the "West Front of the United States Capitol in Washington, D.C." (Wikipedia). January 20, 1989.

(Left) This momerabile is part of mommy's collection is displayed on a glass topped carved wooden table in the formal living room.

Daddy's political career did have some low points. He lost the Senatorial race in 1992, when Salvador "Doy" Laurel, Vice President of Corazon Aquino—11th President of the Philippines—also lost in the Presidential bid in the same election. Daddy was one of the twenty-four senators under the *Nacionalista Party (Laurel-Kalaw ticket)*, garnering 414,061 votes, ranking him as 103 among 165 senatorial bets. Tito Sotto—an entertainer and an athlete-turned-politician—had almost eleven million votes, ranked number one.

An empty lot, where J. Alcantara Street meets Natalio Bacalso Avenue and Leon Kilat Street—the heart of the city— was converted by daddy's construction workers into an instant election platform for Doy and his entourage to campaign.

The well-illuminated stage was decorated, wall to wall, with campaign posters bearing Doy and daddy's grins of victory. Though daddy's victory did not materialize then, his time came three years later, in the smaller, and more personal, political arena of Lawis.

Running for a country's Senatorial seat was a gigantic challenge! Seeing Comelec tabulations, the day after the elections, on TV screens in homes and in business establishments, and on big billboards in the Fuente Osmeña circle and in other strategic areas of the country, showed the enormity of the national race. With less than four percent votes, compared to the highest ranking Senator, daddy's national standing was far from stellar.

I was excited to see his name listed on those giant billboards, among the bigwigs of politics. Daddy and mommy were extremely busy during those times, juggling politics, business, and family all together. But they seemed happy and optimistic.

Daddy also lost in the race for a Congress seat in the May 10, 2001 elections. Had he became a congressman, he could have represented the Fourth District of the province of Cebu, in the House of Representatives, the lower house of the Philippine Congress.

An office staff said that she helped facilitate the selling of *M/V Zenaida*. It was a Japanese marine research boat, (worth a few million Philippine pesos) personally handpicked by daddy in Japan just three years prior. This was to cover for the loss that daddy incurred during the 2001 elections. The new owners supposedly scrapped the ship's body and sold the ship's engine to a shipping company in India. The ship was originally meant to be used for the apprentice experience of the maritime students of SCSIT, the bulk of the school's college students.

Our family visited the ship at least once, during its short stay with us. It was spotless, very well ventilated, and meticulously built, with several lacquered wood panels dividing the walls of the numerous cabins, and beige cotton curtains hung on bronze curtain rods, separating sections of each snug cabin.

The original Japanese marine researchers must have spent a lot of time at sea, considering that there were various sizes of dinnerware in the dining area. Just before the ship was sold, mommy had all the dinnerware brought home. They are now part of mommy's daily table setting.

M/V Zenaida Salazar, Salazar Institute of Technology Laboratory
ship, during the fluvial procession in honor of Senior Sto.
Niño de Cebu at the time when my parents were the 'Hermano and Hermana Mayor.
Her crew were Master Mariner-Capt. Edgar Salgado, 2nd Mate-Artemio Jarina,
AB-Ruel Montaño, Apprentice Mate-Ariel Mancio, Chief Engineer-Abundio
Arevalo, 3rd Engineer-Manolo de la Cerna, 4th Engineer-Alexis
Capuyan, Oiler-Eleser Soco, Aprentice Engineer-Jose Alota
Jr., Ship Electrician-Felix Ysatam. January 2001. (photo credit: Felix Ysatam)

Politics was not the only venue for giving back to the community. As the incumbent President (1979-1982) and Founder of Cebu Contractors

Association, daddy orchestrated the construction of the enormous papal altar in the old Lahug airport, the bustling IT Park today.

A multitude of Catholic devotees, and the former First Lady Mrs. Imelda Marcos, were on hand on February 19, 1981, when Pope John Paul II celebrated Holy Mass on the papal altar constructed by daddy.

In recognition of daddy's efforts, he received a Papal Award - *Pro Ecclesia et Pontifice given on March 29, 1982, through the recommendation of Ricardo Cardinal Vidal. The award was signed by Pope John Paul II.*

A multitude came to celebrate the Holy Mass with Pope John Paul II. The former First Lady Mrs. Imdela Marcos, the "Iron Butterfly", stood on a special area for her on the right of the altar. Her bodyguard stood closely behind her. Imelda is the wife of the former Philippine President Ferdinand Marcos, 10th President of the Philippines. Our family was sitted on the right side, three rows from the front. Cebu City. February 19, 1981.

It was a rainy afternoon. My parents brought the whole family to witness the once-in-a-lifetime event, with the pope visiting the City of Cebu, Philippines—a Third World country. From our seats, several meters away, I witnessed the pope celebrate the Holy Eucharist. He gave First Holy communion to selected young children—one of which was my cousin.

She was dressed in an all-white dress, shoes, and veil. The large crowd opened their umbrellas to shield themselves from the pouring rain. Lovely music was sung by a well-rehearsed choir, accompanied by a full orchestra. It was a heavenly experience.

In spite of his ups and downs in politics, daddy's construction projects kept on going. His feat in construction led President Gloria Macapagal Arroyo, fourteenth president of the Philippines, to appoint him, on September 5, 2005, as a member of the Philippine Contractors Accreditation Board (PCAB) of the Department of Trade and Industry. He took oath on October 11, 2005, in the office of Cebu Governor Gwendolyn Garcia. As a member of PCAB, he and his fellow members were responsible for the building of safe infrastructure in the Philippines.

His appointment as a member of the Philippine Contractors Accreditation Board made him a public servant for the construction industry of the Republic of the Philippines, for the entire nation, and not just for the town of Madridejos, or for the province of Cebu.

Among his multi-million construction projects, these stand out: **Luzon**- Metro Manila: Philippine Long Distance Telephone (PLDT); Philippine Navy Headquarters- Roxas Blvd; Camarines Sur, Bulacan and Mindoro: Regional Manpower Training Centers (RMTC); Pangasinan: Farmers Training Center. **Visayas**- Cebu: Banilad flyover, Carbon Market, Cebu Central School, Channel 9 (Mandaue), National Power Corporation (NPC) Marine works- Naga, Cebu; Philippines National Bank (PNB) Regional Office, Region 7- Jones Avenue, ports (Sta. Fe and Tabuelan), roads (Bantayan and Toledo), Philip Rodriguez residence/shop, Suarez Bros. building. Bohol: roads and bridges. Dumaguete: Development Bank of the Philippines (DBP). Samar: Regional Institute of Fisheries Technology (RIFT)/ Regional Fisheries Training Center (RFTC), roads and bridges. Southern Leyte: PLDT. **Mindanao**- Bukidnon: Kibawe Electric Substation.

One of the "Ten Outstanding Cebuanos". Cebu City. August 20, 2011. (photo credit: Christopher Odtohan)

His outstanding achievements in the field of education was likewise recognized as he became a recipient of the TOCA —the Ten Outstanding Cebuano Award—on August 20, 2011 given by the Engr. Greg Senining, Executive Director of TOCA.

His acceptance speech was impressive, just as his and mommy's achievements were! To add to his laurels, he was awarded Most

Outstanding Civil Engineer of the Philippines for 2013, by the Philippine Institute of Civil Engineers, Inc.

As soon as Lolo Dodóng retired as Dean Emeritus of the College of Engineering, of the University of San Jose Recoletos in the 90s, and his wife, Lola Nena passed on, daddy offered to have him live and work in the SCSIT Cebu Campus. Lolo Dodóng became Dean of all colleges.

Engr. Aurelio Salazar and some of the school staff pose in front of the Dean's office. Early 90s. (photo credit: Teresita "Pompem" Antepuesto Gonzales)

Without any direct heirs, Lolo Dodong was too lonely to live by himself in his original home in Sanciangko Street—the very same place where daddy's spent his late teen-age years as a working scholar. It's very touching to know that the kitchen area of the elementary building was converted into a one-bedroom suite for his ninety-year-old uncle. Lolo Dodong was appointed as the school's first Dean of all Colleges.

Lolo Dodong was quite strict, not just to daddy (as a young man) but also to students and staff. He aimed for perfection in the school documents and demanded professional behaviour of the students and employees in school. As an engineer himself, he was precise and diligent, the very trait adopted by daddy.

"Ka daghan nako'g gipa eskwela, Beth, wala gyuy usa nila nga nibalik ug nagpasalamat nako!" (I sent a lot of youth to school, Beth, not one of them came back to thank me.) Lolo Dodong sighed.

I'm sure a youth or two must have said a little *Thank you* to lolo but he must have failed to recognize it. He was always stern and he looked unapproachable. This did not deter daddy from providing for his last home. The school family became lolo's *family*. The school doctor became his personal doctor. With a wall separating his home and work, lolo was well-taken cared of and well-loved by the school community.

While daddy built a home for his parents in Cebu, he also renovated his in-laws' house in Madridejos. Mommy refurbished her ancestral family home along the north eastern shore of Barangay Poblacion, Madridejos.

It is perfectly situated in a corner lot, facing the seashore and a few minutes drive to the local townhall. Like most homes in town, the front entrance— tucked in the corner of the open porch, surrounded by century-old wooden armchairs, woven with rattan cane webbing for their backrest—lead one to a large living room (for large family gatherings). In the living room, there were several couches and chairs and dotted with wooden cabinets, showcasing antiquated pictures of mommy's family among other souvenir items.

Across the living room was an eight-seater simple wooden dining table, adjacent to the indoor washroom and Lolo Usting's and Lola Bibing's dimly-lighted master bedroom. A door opening (covered by a curtain) connected the master bedroom to lola's dainty corner store. The store was opened only when lola, or anyone else in the family, was able to attend to it. On the right side of the front entrance, there were a few cemented steps leading to a smooth and shiny wooden staircase connecting the ground floor to three medium-sized bedrooms upstairs. The staircase saw the sweat and diligence of mommy's family as they toiled throughout their days (and nights). To this day, her ancestral home gives me lots of lovely memories of my childhood days.

With the bigwigs of Cebu City, Julio Cardinal Rosales, and the former First Lady, Mrs. Imelda Romualdez Marcos. Daddy is 6th from the top left. Mommy is 2nd from the lower left. Basilica del Santo Niño, Cebu City. Late 70s.

My parents connected with public servants to make a change.

Republic of the Philippines
Professional Regulation Commission
Manila

May 16, 2013

ENGR. DOROTEO MONTEDERAMOS SALAZAR
President
SALAZAR COLLEGES OF SCIENCE AND
INSTITUTE OF TECHNOLOGY
211 Natalio Bacalso Avenue
Cebu City

Dear Engr. Salazar:

The Commission extends its warmest congratulations to you for having been chosen as the recipient of the **2013 Outstanding Professional of the Year Award** in the field of **Civil Engineering.**

The **"Outstanding Professional of the Year Award"** is the highest award bestowed by the Commission upon a professional as recommended by his/her peers for having amply demonstrated professional competence of the highest degree and conducted himself/herself with integrity in the exercise of his/her profession, participated meaningfully in professional activities through the professional organization, contributed significantly to the advancement of the profession, and contributed significantly to the effective discharge of the profession's social responsibility through meaningful contribution/participation in socio-related activities.

The awarding ceremonies will be held during the PRC AWARDS NIGHT on June 20, 2013, Thursday, at the Fiesta Pavillion, Manila Hotel, One Rizal Park, Manila. Please be at the venue by 4:00 P.M. for the group picture-taking. The program shall start promptly at 6:00 P.M. You will be given one (1) complementary dinner ticket. Please come in red gown for ladies and black suit with red tie for gentlemen.

We look forward seeing you on this most momentous occasion as you personally receive this most prestigious award.

Once again, our warmest congratulations.

Very truly yours,

TERESITA R. MANZALA
Chairperson

Note: President Aquino to bestow the AWARD.

cc: PICE
Board of Civil Engineering

OC/ASCOM/D-STN
TRM/ATG/CLE/aav

D-STN/2013-05-003/L

P. PAREDES ST., CORNER N. REYES ST., SAMPALOC, MANILA, PHILIPPINES, 1008
P.O. BOX 2038, MANILA

"2013 Outstanding Professional of the Year Award in the field of Civil Engineering".
Given by Philippine Regulation Commission. Daddy's handwriting on the letter shows
that President 'Noynoy' Aquino III bestowed the award. Manila. May 16, 2013.

In appreciation for being Speaker for the Opening Program of the Philippine Institute of Civil Engineers, Inc.'s 39th National Convention. Davao City. November 7, 2013.

The proud couple were warmly welcomed.

Seated in the same Presidential table with President Ferdinant "Bongong" Marcos Jr. (17ᵗʰ and current president of the Philippines (on daddy's left) and the former Philippine President Rodrigo "Digong" Duterte, 16ᵗʰ president of the Philippines (leftmost) . At that time of the PICE Convention, Digong Duterte was Mayor of Davao City. Daddy is second from the right. Davao City. November 7-9, 2013.

PRC's award as "Outstanding Professional of the Year Award in the field of Civil Engineering" brought him national recognition.

Davao City hosts civil engineers' nat'l confab

By Edge Davao · October 6, 2013 3:46 pm

With the theme "Civil Engineering for a Sustainable Future," Davao City will be hosting the Philippine Institute of Civil Engineers (PICE) 39th National Convention on November 7 – 9, 2013 at the SMX Davao Convention Center, Davao City.

This annual convention will be attended by more than 4000 leading members from the construction, consulting, academic and commercial sectors of the government and private offices in the country and abroad.

The Philippine Institute of Civil Engineers (PICE) is a professional organization accredited by the Professional Regulation Commission, composed of more than 73,000 registered civil engineer-members in 97 local and 8 international chapters and some 25,390 civil engineering student-members in 180 student chapters throughout the country.

https://edgedavao.net/the-big-news/2013/10/06/davao-city-hosts-civil-engineers-natl-confab/

Republic of the Philippines
Professional Regulation Commission
Manila

Presents this

Certificate of Appointment

In pursuance to Section 9, Article I of Executive Order No. 496, "Instituting Procedures and Criteria for the Selection and the Recommendation of Nominees for Appointment to Vacant Positions in the Professional Regulatory Boards under the Supervision of the Professional Regulation Commission", and PRC Resolution No. 2013-737 entitled "Creating a Screening Committee Pursuant to Section 9, Article I of Executive Order No. 496, Series of 1991 and Prescribing Guidelines Therefor"

Engr. Doroteo M. Salazar

*is hereby appointed **Vice-Chairman** of the PRB Screening Committee for the Board of Civil Engineering and shall serve for a term until June 16, 2014.*

Issued this 10th day of September, in the year of our Lord, Two Thousand and Thirteen at the Professional Regulation Commission, City of Manila, Philippines.

TERESITA R. MANZALA
Chairperson

JENNIFER JARDIN-MANALILI
Commissioner

(VACANT)
Commissioner

There are other accomplishments too many to mention. My parents had given back to the community as much as their parents had sacrificed for them.

Hebrews 13:16 (ESV)

Do not neglect to do good and to share what you have, for such sacrifices are pleasing to God.

Leviticus 25:35 (ESV) **Kindness for Poor Brothers**

"If your brother becomes poor and cannot maintain himself with you, you shall support him as though he were a stranger and a sojourner

Eight

The Third Floor

Each year I went home, daddy and mommy were always so proud to show me new developments in the school or in our real estate developments.

Thirteen years after the strafing incident, I visited daddy and mommy in May 2017. Daddy was unusually focused on work then. He was not his usual take-it-easy self. He wanted to accomplish something so badly. And he wanted *me* to be part of it.

"Change your dress (clothes) Abet", daddy said seriously.

I *did* change clothes already, but he wanted me to wear something much better, something more professional-looking. This was something he *never* asked me before, even as a little child. I quickly changed into my best attire and

hopped in the car. After a satisfying breakfast of fish—fried, *buwad* (dried) and *tinola* (soup)—with rice and *Nescafe*, Daddy drove mommy and me to school.

We arrived in Madridejos the day before, to visit our school in that town.

He told me earlier that he had invited a V.I.P., an alumna of the maritime department, to visit the campus. And he wanted me to meet her. As soon as I met the lady V.I.P. I was excited to know that she was the first female ship captain of the Cebu Ports Authority, quite a significant achievement for her and for our school. She was introduced to the rest of the staff in school, then we took her for a tour around the major areas of the school. My parents were very happy to show her around the campus.

Once in a while daddy invited dignitaries to our school for several reasons: to guide our school staff with numerous government requirements and to establish connections. Since Madridejos is the only town with a private college, the presence of a dignitary in the campus puts our place on the map.

The day after the V.I.P. left the campus, daddy had his usual meeting with the members of the Executive Board of the school, composed of the deans and department heads of all colleges and departments. These meetings are usually an hour long and are done around 5pm.

That meeting lasted longer than usual, when the moon and the stars were seen in the heavens, when the staff were uneasy, tired, and restless, including mommy.

Rrrrrrring! Rrrrrrring! Rrrrrrring!

Daddy's phone rang quietly. After a quick glance of his phone, he dropped the call. It rang again a few more times but he dropped the calls again. Mommy had given him many signals to end his meeting. She was seated at the front row among the participants. Since I sat beside her, I noticed mommy's frustration on her face. I looked behind me and saw several weary-looking eyes looking back at me. I heard staff shifting on their seats, all eager to get up at the first sound of dismissal. In fact, a few, slowly sneaked out of the door.

Filipino culture respects authority. During those school meetings, verbal participation was minimal, unless something urgent was discussed. At that particular meeting, daddy did *all* of the talking, from past accomplishments, to reminders, to future plans and projects of the school—something quite significant to the school—but best heard with active, rested, and receptive ears, and a full belly.

At about five thirty in the afternoon, daddy finally dismissed the group. The attendees quickly got up and left the room. Mommy and I lingered as daddy was still chatting with a few personnel outside the meeting place. He was beaming with deep self-accomplishment, as if telling the world that he was satisfied with the words he shared with his employees, the words which would move the institution towards the direction he envisioned.

Back in the main island of Cebu, and in the main campus of the school, the administration building was reaching its half century mark, built in the late 60s. The original design was an L-shaped two storey building which used to house the students' canteen, the offices of the Dean, Registrar, Accounting, Executive Management, Board Room, on the ground floor, and Review classrooms on the second floor. When the Salazar Engineering Review Center was transformed into a school, classrooms were converted into management offices, more classrooms, computer laboratories, and other functional areas, while improving the interior design and educational environment.

Across the Administration Building was the bigger five-storey building housing the high school students and other college courses. It was equipped with classrooms, offices, and laboratories fitted to provide quality education while meeting government requirements.

With combined yearly enrollment figures creeping up to seven thousand, for both the Cebu and Madridejos campuses, daddy decided to add a third floor to the administration building. As the Project Engineer himself, he supervised the foreman and laborers to do the job.

At the age of eighty one, he was still able to climb the temporary wooden stairs leading to the upper floor. Every time daddy went up the ladder, the lead foreman made sure that he made it up safety. As usual mommy stayed in the office to look into the school finances.

To add to the strength of the building, daddy changed the wooden flooring of the second floor to make it concrete. His engineering prowess was once again put to use, from the planning, foundation, framing and finishing phases of the construction.

I was terrified to see him go up the make-shift stairs, holding the wooden make-shift handle, briskly. Cecile reminded us that he should use a head covering to shield himself from the thirty plus heat of the tropical sun. But, strong-willed as he was, he refused. Dark skin pigmentation on his face and hands could have been early signs of skin cancer. Although he had gone up and down in several of his construction projects spanning six decades, his age and physical well-being did not seem fit to do that job anymore. Nevertheless, he finished the third floor around the summer of that year.

A few days before I was leaving for Canada, we had a poolside dinner in *Casino Español*, mommy's favorite place, where we got first class service and full attention from the servers. We had *lengua* (ox tongue), *grilled tanguige* (Spanish mackerel), *sinigang soup* (Filipino sour soup), Four Seasons juice, Nature Spring bottled water, and steamed plain rice, while a string band played traditional Filipino music in the background. Time was well spent with my parents in this cool summer evening.

On the day of my departure, we had lunch in a native restaurant inside Mactan airport. Daddy had soup again and mommy and I had fish with rice. We heard clinking and clanking of spoons and forks against cups, bowls, and plates, while busy travelers were dining with family, friends and acquaintances, awaiting their boarding time.

Meals with daddy and mommy were usually quiet. While I was chewing on my *fried bangus* (milkfish) and sipping my cold mango juice, I could not help but think about the next time I would have a meal with them again. Mommy looked perfectly fine, eating well, and being her usual self. But daddy looked really haggard, as seen in the family pictures of Baba's (his great grand daughter) second birthday in *Jollibee* (Filipino multinational chain of fast food restaurants).

I had a deep fear that *that* moment would be so special, that *that* meal would be so precious, even if it was just thirty minutes together, so memorable, so unforgettable. I savoured every moment. The fear of losing a parent was gripping my heart unbidden.

"I have to board my plane *na* (already)", I bid a quick farwell, as I looked hurriedly into their eyes. I was afraid of bursting into tears so I *blessed* their hands, hurriedly carried my backpack, and got up to pull my luggage. My chest tightened, then…. uncontrollable tears were falling. I kept on going through my tear-filled vision.

"*Nihilak man siya,*" (She cried.) mommy sadly observed.

"*Gi mingaw ra na nato.*"(She just misses us.) daddy replied.

I overheard them say those words while I still saw them from the corner of my eye. They were seated by the third table, by the doorless entrance, their backs against the wall, drinking the last sip from their water glasses. They looked at me over their right shoulder, as I was getting ready to leave.

I didn't look back. I kept on going, for fear of losing my composure in public.

I continued to drag my luggage towards the pre-departure area, holding back more tears. *I had to be strong and composed.* I was only thirty seven hours away from my foreign adopted home.

Little did I know that I would be back to Cebu in less than a month—not having a poolside meal with my parents in *Casino Español* but in a bedside meal with daddy at *Chong Hua Hospital*. The fear gave way to reality. July 23, 2017 was the day he passed on.

Daddy's favorite song was *My Way*, popularized by Frank Sinatra in 1969—the years when daddy and mommy were ascending towards the peak of their careers. The pop song is about self-determination, about dealing with the challenges of life while walking towards one's sunset years. As daddy faced the final curtain, mommy had been gracefully coping, for awhile, until…she faced her final curtain too, six years later on April 28, 2023.

A mother and daugther lunch . Lantaw Native Restaurant, South Road Properties, Cebu CIty. December 2019.

Hallways leading to change, SCSIT Cebu Campus, June 2023.

Psalm 71:18 (ESV)

So even to old age and gray hairs,
    O God, do not forsake me,
until I proclaim your might to another generation,
    your power to all those to come.

Job 1:21(ESV)

And he said, "Naked I came from my mother's womb, and naked shall I return. The LORD gave, and the LORD has taken away; blessed be the name of the LORD."

2 Corinthians 4:16-18 (ESV)

So we do not lose heart. Though our outer self[a] is wasting away, our inner self is being renewed day by day. For this light momentary affliction is preparing for us an eternal weight of glory beyond all comparison, as we look not to the things that are seen but to the things that are unseen. For the things that are seen are transient, but the things that are unseen are eternal.

Letter to the Reader

Join us in continuing the legacy of education started by Dodo and Naiding. Their dream to put up Salazar Colleges of Science and Institute of Technology (SCSIT) as a non-profit, non-stock organization has come to fruition.

The next chapter of the school is to continue to support the scholars of Dodo and Naiding, improve the school facilities, construct a covered court/gym, purchase updated library collections, and upgrade the professional development of our faculty members and staff.

As an institution of basic education and higher learning, SCSIT had been serving the poor and disadvantaged students of the community for over 40 years. Donations from public or private individuals or organizations are highly appreciated.

Please visit our website for further information at:
http://scsit.edu.ph/

Epilogue

Daddy and mommy's school Salazar Colleges of Science and Institute of Technology celebrated it's 40th Founding Anniversary on February 4, 2023 with the theme: **Reflecting 40th Resilient Years.**

Daddy authored an article in the school publication, 2012.

Several graduates and relatives are grateful for the education and accommodation given to them. Here are a few messages from them:

HONORABLE ENGR. ROMEO A. VILLACERAN
Madridejos Mayor (May 12, 2022 to present)
Previous Barangay Captain, Barangay Ma-alat, Mardridejos, Cebu
Previous Working Student as Janitor, SIT, 1983-1988
Previous Project Engineer, Salazar Construction Co. Inc., 1989-1997

While doing an interview for a video, October 2021. (photo/video credit: Marvelous Madridejos-YouTube)

"Ni graduate ko mam 1988 sa college didto ko ni graduate highskol sa madridejos national high school.. sa 1982 wala pay gi offer nga civil engineering sa SIT so diha ko nag working sa inyo pero didto ko gi pa eskuela ni sir dodo sa cit kay may konektion pa sa una si sir dodo sa cit diha man sya ni graduate as king og engineer and summa cum laude unya after ana diha ko nag review sa inyo salazar review center."

I graduated college in 1988. I graduated high school in Madridejos National High School in 1982. Since Civil Engineering was not yet offered in SIT, I worked with your parents. Sir Dodo requested me to study in CIT while he still had connections there at that time. It was also in CIT where he graduated King of Engineers and summa cum laude. After that I reviewed in your Salazar Review Center.

"Si sir dodo ang nag bayad sa una sa akoa tuition sa college sa cit after graduation. Dha nako nag review sa salazar review center 1988 to 1990. Then pag take nako og board exam nov 1990 kalooy sa dios ni pasar ko pagka civil egineer
This is my life... I almost ur daddy's life working student with the help of ur family. Then became licensed civil engineer, contractor with multi million project,then brgy captain, then presently mayor of madridejos . I dedicate this life to my idol MAYOR ENGR DOROTEO MONTEDERAMOS SALAZAR"

Sir Dodo paid for my college tuition in CIT. After graduation I reviewed at Salazar Review Center (from) 1988 to 1990. When I took the board exam in November 1990, with the mercy of God, I passed it and became a Civil Engineer. This is my life.... I owe it to your daddy. I became a working student with the help of your family. I became a licensed Civil Engineer, a Contractor with multi-million projects, then a Barangay Capitan, then presently Mayor of Madridejos.

"Hehe og dili tungod sa imong amahan dili sad ko mahimo ing ani ako gyod to sya idol."

Hehehe if not for your dad, I could not have been what I am today. He is really my idol.

August 31, 2021, Madridejos, Bantayan Island, Cebu, Philippines.

Romeo replied to my Facebook message on August 31, 2021, as I congratulated him as Maalat's (a *barangay* of Madridejos) Barangay Capitan. Finally during the May 9, 2022 mayoral elections, Romeo became Mayor of Madridejos, five years after daddy texted him.

DR. DANILO G. GUDELOSAO
Assistant Schools Division Superintendent (2014 to present)
Department of Education SIT Alumus
BSED major in Mathematics Pioneering Batch 1991.
Previous Working Student as Property Custodian, SIT, 1987-1991.

With mommy and Dr. Serapion Sotto, School Director, SCSIT Administration Office, Cebu Campus, 2018.

"Salazar Institute of Technology was an unexpected surprise gift to me when I was informed that I was one of the recipients of the Cardinal Vidal Scholarship Program way back in 1987. After my high school graduation, pursuing college education was impossible for me due to lack of financial resources. Though I was only required to pay P5.00 every semester for the

scholarship form, a bigger challenge was on my daily sustenance. Thanks to the generousity of Engr. Doroteo "Dodo" Monte de Ramos Salazar and Mrs. Zenaida Fuguracion Salazar for I was given the opportunity to work as one of the school's Administrative Staff as Property Custodian with monthly stipend until college graduation. Engr. Salazar inspired me as he personally related to me his struggles, sacrifices and determination as a college work-scholar at the Cebu Institute of Technology, graduated BS Civil Engineering Suma Cum Laude, King of Engineers and Board Topnotcher. After my college graduation, I worked as a high school teacher in SIT for six years. A bigger door of opportunities unfolded when I started working at the Department of Education. I brought with me the best years of teaching experience, friendship, values and the personal influence of Engr. Salazar on me. Had it not for Engr. Doroteo M. Salazar and the Salazar Institute of Technology (SIT), now the Salazar College of Science and Institute of Technology (SCSIT), I would not have achieved my colorful journey as a teacher, a leader and a public servant. For all of these, my loyalty and gratefulness remain."

January 6, 2023. Cebu City, Philippines.

ENGR. FREDERICK BAISAC SUICO

Production Manager, Conduent Business
Services Inc., a BPO company, Cebu City,
handling a healthcare account
supervising almost 300 staff.
High School General Curriculum
    Batch '86
1st Honorable Mention
Grammarian of the Year
3rd Place - Copyreading and Headline
    Writing - Divisional Secondary
    Press
Conference
7th Place - Sports Writing - Regional
Secondary Press Conference
Associate in Civil Engineering
    Batch '88
Academic Awardee

SUICO, FREDERICK B.
56 bf Pacaña St., Tisa, Cebu City
October 21, 1969
To be a successful Physical
Therapist.

Ricric was studying in Pope John XXIII Minor Seminary in Cebu in 1984 when his father was retrenched from his job at Atlas Consolidate Mining and Development Corporation in Toledo, Cebu. Since his father could not support his studies, his parents looked for a school with affordable tuition. They decided to consider SIT.

In 1984, the second year of the opening of Salcon Institute of Technology, all high school year levels, from first to fourth year, were opened. The first and second years offered both the General and Technical curriculum, while the third and fourth year only had the General curriculum. Ricric was enrolled in third year and Dahlia, his sister, in second year. Jake, their younger brother enrolled in first year high school the following year.

He was part of the pioneer third year high school in SIT with Madam Adoracion Lawawan as his adviser in section Bonfacio. There were about 50-60 students in third year, split between the Rizal and Bonifacio sections.

"Then nag officer ko sa CAT. I was S2 at that time." Then I was the Corps S2/ Intelligence officer in CAT (Citizens Army Training) at that time.

After Ricric graduated high school in 1986, he continued his studies in SIT taking Associate in Civil Engineering, a two year course leading to a Bachelor of Science in Civil Engineering (BSCE).

"We were the first batch of engineering students in SIT (Cebu campus). At that time Civil, Mechanical and Electrical engineering were offered. There was about 40 of us in total."

"All college students nag fieldtrip mi sa Madridejos as part sa among curriculum observing road repair sa Bantayan when it was handled by Salcon." As part of our curriculum, all college students had a field trip to Madridejos, to observe the repair of the roads from the town of Bantayan to the town of Madridejos. It was a project of Salcon (Salazar Construction Co. Inc.).

"This is an iconic and so memorable photo. We were among the first batch of college students (Associate in Civil Engineering) of 1988. Along with Jerwin Abellar, we are the only ones who were from high school who entered college when it opened its doors to the first collegiate education. This was even before Bantayan college opened. I was also the first academic awardee for the first associate graduation."

Since SIT did not offer BSCE then, Ricric (with his high school classmate, Jerwin) proceeded with his degree at the Cebu Institute of Technology. After they graduated, they took the civil engineering board exams and passed. *"Jerwin and I passed the board exams."*

"Dili gyud ko kalimot nag working ko" I will never forget that I was a working student. *"that time under the supervision of the late Engr. Aurelio Salazar. I was distributing chemistry department materials as controller."* ☺

"Si Sir Aurelio is the silent type medyo stricto ug dating pero he has a very good heart. Daghan to siya natabangan working student." Sir Aurelio was the strict and silent type, but he has a very good heart. He helped many

working students. *He was the one who approved that I will be* assigned in the *chemistry dept. If my memory serves me right, Sir Aurelio was the school Director."*

"Si Sir Doroteo commanding kaau ug dating mataha mi kay King of Engrs. Pero imong daddy always smiles sa students. Buotan kaayo." Sir Doroteo had a commanding presence since he was King of Engineers. But he always had a smile for students. He was very kind.

"Your mom is very beautiful. Yes she is, pero medyo strict si maam hehe." Your mom is very beautiful, yes she was, but she was a bit strict.

"I remember Romeo Villaceran (future Madridejos Mayor) and Camlon (trusted SIT employee) too hehe."

"I have fond memories of the founder couple. SIT Intrams 1985, they were my first marriage booth subjects. I was the bogus officiating priest 😁."

Celebrating 15 years anniversary of his team as Production Manager, Conduent, Cebu. September 2023.

I informed Ricric that I will include him in the Epilogue of my book. *"wow write-up in SIT book, I would be very proud. Hehehe uwawa ma feature pero (it's embarrassing to be featured but) its time to return the favor to my alma mater"*

Below is a link to the SIT Salcon Batch 1983-1987 reunion on September 9, 2023.

https://www.facebook.com/watch/?v=218417614246719

August 31, 2023. Cebu City, Philippines

MS. GRACE ALLANIC ZABALA

Nurse for aged care facilty with
Queensland Health,
Queensland, Australia
Nominated for Pride of Workmanship
Award of the Rotary Club of Taupo
New Zealand, 2012
Masters in Business Management,
University of the Philippines,
Cebu City, 2001
Pioneer General Curriculum High
School Batch '87
Class Valedictorian

*Grace (middle), in the company of
her Australian colleagues at work.*

Grace was just eleven years old, an elementary graduate of Labangon Elementary School, Cebu City, when her neighbor, Josephine Chua (also a pioneer graduate), informed her about **Salcon Institute of Technology (SIT)**.

SIT just opened that schoolyear, June 1983, a new school in their neighborhood.

Her young parents had financial difficulties at that time so she wanted to go to a school who accepted underprivileged students. With the help of her neighbor's parents, she enrolled at SIT. Since she always topped in class, she became full scholar throughout her four years in high school, paying only P20.00 upon entrance.

Grace was nominated for the "Pride of Workmanship Award", by the Rotary Club of Taupō, New Zealand (Taupō Weekender. 2012), for her exemplary care and compassion for the Liston Heights Residential Care facility in Taupō, New Zealand.

"So thankful timing kaayu ang SIT ni open doors for people like me. (So thankful and very timely that SIT opened doors for people like me."

It was perfect timing that SIT opened its doors to people like me.

Although she had no particular favorite teacher, all of them were very important to her. I chatted with her through Facebook messenger on August 19, 2023 while she was on night duty:

maam lanawan and maam abarquez gave me the opportunity to grow towards writing
by taking me to the secondary schools press conference
but I understood that it was Sir Dodo who also pushed for the school to be
represented coz we needed budget to get there regionally and we won!

"but other activities that i have experienced helped a lot: Sir Basul (rip) and Sir Sevilla in CAT training

I gained so much confidence in leadership skills."

I feel really proud of our school even though it's not one of the usual "sikat" (famous) schools in Cebu.

I was the SIT (high school) valedictorian but no honors from the Elem school.

I was hardworking student very active and involved in a lot of things in high school.

I have always felt the passion to also give to the underprivileged"

In our earlier conversation I asked Grace: I would like to know if you remember what my late dad Pres Salazar said about why he opened the school. This was her reply on Facebook messenger:

"Hello Mam Beth. Thanks for asking. I cannot remember word-for-word when the late President of SIT was speaking to us but I do have vivid memories of him on the podium as I grew-up with the school he invested his time and energy on."

"In my heart it was all about Engr. Doroteo M. Salazar's mission to provide education for the masses.

He opened it with the welcoming arms for us who have completed elementary school but would not have the access to other secondary schools due to various reasons. He made it accessible for children like me and from all walks of life. We were given opportunity to start our secondary education without the pressure from having no financial capability (which was my case), and others' would be due to being unable to fulfil the requirements to the other schools.

He made it an education that is reachable for anybody and anyone who were willing to study, and also to those who needed a second chance.

He was a very generous person! He was willing to provide scholarship to some of his students. I will have to add the fact that I am so grateful and felt honoured to be one of his pioneer students, and I wish I have not failed his dreams of giving a brighter future for us who were not very privileged.

I know in my heart that the successes I achieved in my life now was due to Sir Salazar's drive and enthusiasm to provide the education that we needed. I have been given the biggest opportunity in my young life to continue with my studies in his school as a full scholar starting from the first year of high school and up until I completed. I am actually trying to find a way to express my gratitude to him and with this I hope that it shall reach to all who may want to know his legacy.

I do get emotional Mam Beth, and it has been so long with all the trials in life I have not been able to see him prior to his passing but in my heart I feel his work and contribution to humanity. Maybe that is why ever since I came to live in New Zealand to immigrate, I always give to all kinds of charity groups because I know exactly how it can make a huge difference to a person's life.

I had post-grad study sa Univ of Auckland coz goal was to do Masters in Health Sciences (as per recommendations from my nurse director at the time in Taupo Hospital in NZ) which was funded by the health workers union.

But then I decided to stop only up to Graduate Certificate level and focused on travel-nursing in Australia.

I am now working in Queensland, Australia and still a NZ citizen."
July 28, 2021. Queensland, Australia

MRS. H. A. A.

Public School Elementary Teacher, Naga, Cebu, Philippines, 1999 to present

Previous Elementary Teacher, SIT, 1991-1999

Department of Education SIT Alumus

BSED major in Mathematics Pioneering Batch 1991.

Awarding ceremony at her work, early 2000s.

"He's one of the angels sent by God to answer my prayers which is to finish my college education."

"Tungod sa among kalisud mam beth d na gyd ko gustong mangguna sa bukid. Sige gyd kog ampo nga makaeskwela gyd kog college dn ni abot si engineer sa amo school dn ddto nagsugod ang tanan. Nahuman gyd ko."

Due to financial hardships, I used to remove the weeds of our farm. I kept on praying that I will be able to go to college. Then an engineer visited our school. That was how it started. I was finally able to finish college.

"Mam sa asturias man ko nag hi school dn college sit batch 91. Kami pioneer sa educ mam. Nagschool to school campaign man to sila mam. Ni offer silag scholarship sa valedictorian ug salutatorian."

I finished high school in Asturias (Cebu). Danny (Gudelusao) and I were in the same Education batch. There was a school-to-school campaign. The (personnel who visited our school) offered to give scholarships to valedictorians and salutatorians.

Since Mrs. H. A. A. was a valedictorian, she was qualified for the scholarship. She paid P5.00 per semester.

"Mam Beth gd morning. Thank you soooo much for remembering me and reaching me out."

August 28, 2021, Naga, Cebu, Philippines.

JIMWELL TORION

Sports Development Officer, Department of Agriculture, Municipal of Argao, Cebu

Philippine Basketball Association (PBA) player 2000-2007.

Selected by the Batang Red Bull Engergizers as Point guard.

MVP Final for the Philippine Basketball League (PBL)

Rookie of the Year, SIT Skyblazers men's basketball team, 1991-1995.

SIT High School Alumnus Batch 1995

ENGR. ELY D. CATAMCO

Consultant Textile Development,

Top Management's Steering Committee Member, Fakir Fashion Limited, Dhaka,

Bangladesh

Previous Assistant Project Manager Salazar Construction Co. Inc., 1981-1983

Previous Private Residence Security Guard, 1977-1981

"Sugod ko Private SG direct sa inyo 1977 kay nag trabaho ko sa usa ka security agency gi assigned ko sa inyong balay 1976 pa and after a year gi offer ni daddy mo (Engr. Dodo Salazar) kuhaon ko niya as Private guard sa inyoha mao gi accept nako ang offer from that time direct ako sweldo sa SALCON Office until naka graduate ko sa BSChE, unya ga review ko sa SRC sa instruction sa imong daddy. Mao nga na Professional Chemical Engineer ako 1982."

I started as a private security guard with your family in 1977. The year before that I worked for a security agency who assigned me to your home. A year later your daddy (Engr. Dodo Salazar) offered me to work directly for him. I accepted the offer. From that time on I was paid directly by SALCON Office. Upon the instructions of your daddy, I reviewed with Salazar Review Center until I became a Professional Chemical Engineer in 1982.

MR. HILARIO (ELY) DECENA CATAMCO
CONSULTANT TEXTILE DEVELOPMENT
FAKIR FASHION LIMITED

(Above) During a company affair in Pakistan. 1991-1995. (Right) Featured in Ely's last job before he retired in Metro Manila, Philippines. late 2022.

"Dako kaayo ang gikatabang ni daddy(Engr. Salazar) nimo sa akong pag ka ako karon."

Your daddy (Engr. Salazar) helped me so much to become who I am today.

"Year 1983 mi resigned ko gi ingnan ko imong daddy nga I have to practice my profession as a Chemical Engineer kay may offer ko sa usa Chemical Plant sa Calamba Laguna. Mao tong tuiga nga na lain ang ako trabaho from Civil to Chemical practice but I nurtured the lesson I've learned in the Civil Engineering field though I am already a Polymer Engineer sa usa ka Nylon Mfg Plant sa Manila."

In 1983 I was given a job offer to work for a Chemical Plant in Calamba Laguna. When I informed your daddy about my offer he said that I have to practice my profession as a Chemical Engineer. That was the year that I changed my profession from a Civil to Chemical. But I've nurtured the lessons I've learned in the Civil Engineering field though I am already a Polymer Engineer in a Nylon Manufacturing Plant in Manila.

"In silence, I am expressing my heartfelt gratitude to him and your whole family."

Ely's achievement was feature in a brochure of the company in Pakistan where he last worked.

January 30, 2022, Rodriguez, Rizal, Philippines.

MRS. JAURES MACAPOBRES NEGRE
Niece of Mrs. Zenaida Figuracion Salazar
(From the Lolo Julian Figuracion
    Clan, younger
brother of Lolo Usting, father of
    mommy)

"Tita Naiding, Thank you for your countless deeds of kindness, love and care without expecting any favors in return to Figuracion clan, especially to JULIAN CLAN. You allowed mom Erna to build a small house in your vacant lot at the City, by the hi way where we all stayed and finished college. This was before building an extension for SIT college

Bachelor of Science in Biology (Velez College), 1986, Bachelor of Science in Physical Therapy (SWU), 1989, SWU, Cebu City, Philippines.

school. We all had great, priceless memories. Until today we keep on talking about the fun and experiences we had during those days. You will forever be cherished. In behalf of my family Julian clan and my siblings Eternal rest grant unto Tita Naiding oh Lord and let your perpetual light shine upon her and May she rest in peace. Amen🙏🙏🙏."

April 29, 2023, (as posted on Facebook)

"Nagpasalamaton kami ug dako nga gipapoyo kami nga libre sa inyo yuta sa likod sa SIT school hangtod kami nahuman tanan nga mga pag umangkon(tanan tanan gayod as in, kang Lolo Julian clan from Lawis) before nila gigamit ang area para add ug building sa school . Dili namo sila makalimtan sa ilang pagka supportive, ilang mga advices para sa future. Labi na ang advice nga mag TINABANGAY gayod kung kinsa to ang nag lisod tabangan. Ang imo dad ang advice nga mag invest, mag open ug business sa Lawis para makatabang sa lungsod. Advice nila nga poro sa maayong ka ugmaon ug tabang sa naglisod".

We are very grateful that we were given the chance to live for free in a piece of land at the back of SIT school until all of us (nieces and nephews from the clan of Lolo Julian from Lawis (Madridejos) finished college. This was before they used the area to add a building for the school. We will never forget their (daddy and mommy) support and advices for the future. They advised us to help each other especially those who need help the most. Your daddy advised that we invest in a business in Lawis (Madridejos) to help the town. Both of them gave advices for a good future and to help those who are in hardships.

January 12, 2023, Mobile, Alabama, USA

FORMER TEACHERS AND STAFF CELEBRATE DADDY'S 80th BIRTHDAY!

They suprised daddy on his 80th birthday, February 4, 2016.

Behind the scene, the celebration continues! (photo credit: Eunice Fernandez Pactol, working scholar, graduated Bachelor of Science in Education, Major in Mathematics, March 1996, Elementary teacher 1999-2009.)

Daddy's 87ʰ birthday celebration, Founders' Week, SCSIT Cebu Campus. February 2023. (photo credit: Jojo Teves)

(Above left) Mommy meeting special guests during college graduation while Dr. Sotto stands behind her, April 2018. (Above right) Rare moment when mommy addresses an audience. Founders' Week 2018, the year after daddy passed. SCSIT Cebu Campus. (Lower left) Mommy smiles while holding my Christmas gift for her. (Lower right) Walking across the beachfront of Salazar Sunset Beach Resort, Tarong, Madridejos.

Mommy's last "Pasko sa SCSIT" (Christmas in SCSIT),
Cebu City campus, December 2022.

"The flag is raised at half-mast as the school mourns the passing of our dearest mother, Zenaida
Fugracion Salazar, April 29, 2023" (photo credit: SCSIT - Madridridejos Facebook page)

The Municipality of Madridejos Condoles with the Salazar Family
April 29, 2023

"The Municipality of Madridejos Condoles with the Salazar Family April 29, 2023 The Municipality of Madridejos condoles with the Salazar family on the passing of the former Mayor and Vice Mayor of the Municipality of Madridejos and Co-founder of the Salazar Colleges of Science and Institute of Technology, Zenaida Figuracion Salazar. She ushered the beginnings of tourism in the town by spearheading the construction of the welcome arch, planting of trees along the entrance arch, beautification of the town plaza, and the conversion of the old patio cemetery to Kota Heritage Park. She was a vital part of the team that won the "Gawad Kalinga ("to give care" in Tagalog) Clean and Green Award" for Madridejos. May she rest in peace" *(SCSIT - Madridridejos Facebook page)*

Ecclesiastes 3 ESV
A Time for Everything

3 For everything there is a season, and a time for every matter under heaven:
[2] a time to be born, and a time to die;
a time to plant, and a time to pluck up what is planted;
[3] a time to kill, and a time to heal;
a time to break down, and a time to build up;
[4] a time to weep, and a time to laugh;
a time to mourn, and a time to dance;
[5] a time to cast away stones, and a time to gather stones together;
a time to embrace, and a time to refrain from embracing;
[6] a time to seek, and a time to lose;
a time to keep, and a time to cast away;
[7] a time to tear, and a time to sew;
a time to keep silence, and a time to speak;
[8] a time to love, and a time to hate;
a time for war, and a time for peace.
https://biblehub.com/esv/ecclesiastes/3.htm

Appendix 1

**Transcript of Dr. Doroteo Salazar's Acceptance Speech
As TOCA Awardee, Field of Education**
(with English translation from the Cebuano dialect)

Awarded by: Engr. Greg Senining, Executive Director of TOCA
When: August 20, 2011
Where: Sacred Heart Center, D. Jakosalem St., Cebu City, Philippines

Standing Proud! Cebu City. August 20, 2011. (photo credit: Chris Odtohan)

Part 1:

...*kuha sa tanang storya sa awardees nga akong buskuson sa sinco minutos. Igo na nga kamo nakakita nila, ug nabatian ang ilang nahimo, kay abotan tag kadlawon ug atong hisgutan kada usa, ug unsay ilang nahimo. (clears his throat)*

... get all of the stories which I will summarize in five minutes. It is enough that you see them, and you heard what they have done, since it will take until dawn if we talk about each one, and what each one had done. (clears his throat)

Pagkabasa sa akong apo nga usa ko's mga awardees as Outstanding Cebuano, nangutana siya nako, 'Papa, why are you awarded as an Outstanding Cebuano?' Kamo ray tubag niana. Sayon ra gyud kaayo. Tungod tingali, kay I am out, ug sa akong edad still standing, that's why I am outstanding! (audience laughs)

When my grandson read that I was one of the awardees for Outstanding Cebuano, he asked me. "Papa, why are you awarded as an Outstanding Cebuano?" You can answer that by yourself. It's very easy. It's probably because I am out, then, because of my age, still standing, that's why I am outstanding! (audience laughs)

Ika duha, ang atong kinabuhi, gi bahin sa lawas sa tao, ubos sa tiyan, tungod sa tiyan, ug ibabao sa tiyan. Ubos sa tiyan, ang imong pagkabatan-on. Tungod sa tiyan, tungod sa middle age naka. Ug above sa tiyan nga ibabao ka na gyod sa middle age. (audience lightly giggles)

Second, our life is divided into the body of a person, below the belly, near the belly, and above the belly. Below the belly is your youth. Near the belly, because you are already middle aged. And above the belly when you are really above middle age. (audience lightly giggles)

Unsa may imong ma-ilhan nga ang tao middle age na? Kay duna nakay award para niini. Daghan nakag nahimo sa kinabuhi pero ang kinadak-ang testimoni ug testigos sa imong pagka middle age kay ang imong tiyan mo dako-dako naman. (audience laughs). Mao nay middle aged.

What is your sign of a man in his middle age? If you have an award for this, you have done many things in life. But the biggest testimony and witness of your being middle aged is the size of your growing belly. (audience laughs) That is middle age.

Ug ang imong kinabuhi ug imong financial standard naa naka sa ginganlan sa Pilipinas ug middle-income bracket, may trabaho, may pangita, pero usahay, sa middle of the month, wa nakay kwarta, mang huwam kas middle man. (audience giggles) *Mao ni ang atong kinabuhi sa Pilipinas.*

And your life and financial standard is what is called in the Philippines as middle-income bracket, with work, with income, but at times, in the middle of the month, you run out of money, you borrow from the middle man. (audience giggles) That is life in the Philippines.

Akong balikon, kining atong mga awardees, dili na kinahanglan tukion ang ilang nahimo ug nahatag sa katawhan pero nagpahimangno ra ko ninyo.

I will repeat, for these awardees, we do not need to examine what they have done or have given to the people, but I have some reminders for you.

Sa akong pagka estudyante, hantud sa akong paka professional, pagka contractor, pagka mayor, hantud karon, nakit-an nako ang tinuod nga kinabuhing pilipinhon, uban sa among nakita sa pagsuroy suroy sa tibu-ok kalibutan.

As a student, until I became a professional, as a contractor, as a mayor, until today, I have seen the real Filipino life, including what we saw as we traveled throughout the world.

Niadtung Domingo didto pa mis Japan kay na disgrasya akong apo naminyo ug Haponesa. Nganong na disgrasya? Traynta minutos mi nag atubang sa akong mga in-laws, di gyud mi magka estoryahay. (audience giggles) *Unsa-on pagestorya nila? Sila di ka antigog ininglis, kami sab di ka antigog Japanese. Wa gyud mi tingog tingog. Sigi lang mig yango-yango. (audience laughs).*

Last Sunday we were in Japan since my grandson had accidentally married a Japanese. Why an accident? For thirty minutes we were facing our in-laws, without talking to each other. (audience giggles) How could we talk? They cannot speak English, we cannot speak Japanese. We did not make any sound. We just kept on nodding at each other.

Now we come to education, before we will go to that, kay mo hisgut pud ko sa akong pagka mayor, garbo kaayo namo nga Bantayan maoy naghimo gyud nga naay kindak-ang poultry. Unya gani naka imbinto mi og pormula nga kana among poultry record sa manok dagko ug gahi pa iyang shell, mao na nga sa mayor pako, mo singgit ang taga Taboan, nga ang inyong paliton itlog, kadtong itog ni Salazar kay dagko na, gahi pa. (audience laughs out loud and lightly applauds). Mao nay among tirada didto sa Bantayan.

Now we come to education. Before we will go into that, I will also talk about my being a mayor. We are proud to have Bantayan as the biggest source of poultry (farms). Well, we invented a formula to make the chicken eggshell big and hard. That is why when I was mayor, those in *Taboan* (market) would tell the crowd to buy the eggs of Salazar, which are big and hard. (audience laughs out loud). That was our aim there in Bantayan.

Ang akong (voice rising) gi pangutana kaninyong tanan, sa among na obserbahan, bisan kamo, dili man kay kini ra, maoy awardee, kitang tanan awardee, ha. Lingi-a ra gud ang atong mga barangay ug mga lungsod, unsay kaugmaon, sa atong mga batan-on. (whispers). Ako ning hanigan sa statistics.

My question to all of you, in my observation, and yours, these are not the only awardee(s). We are all awardee(s),(expression of emphasis). Look at our *barangays* and towns: what is the future of our youth? I will support this with statistics.

Twenty three million Philippine youths are schooled, are enrolled in schools. There are 2,180 colleges and universities all over the Philippines.

Daghan pa tag eskwelahan sa tibuok United States.
We have more schools than all of the United States.

Dinhi sa Region 7, ang tanan natong eskelahan, sento seysintay uno. Tresi ra gyuy dili public sa colleges. Ang tanan puros private. Mahibaw-an ug unsay participation sa private. Kini niang mga estudyante, sa mo eskwela sa grade one, ang mo eskwelag usa ka gatos sa grade one, ang mo gradwar sa grade six, (pauses and looks at his notes) mo enroll sa high school kwarentay tres ra ka buok, out of 100.

Here in Region 7, we have 161 schools. Only 13 are not public colleges. The rest are private. We will see the participation of the private. These students who study grade one, those 100 who go to grade one, and then graduate grade 6, (pauses and looks at his notes), only 43 out of 100 will enroll in high school .

Ug ni aning kwarentay tres, ang mo graduar sa college, baynti uno. Sa usa ka gatos, baynti uno ang ni graduar sa college. Asa naman ang sitintay nuebe? Kadaghanan niana tingali na enroll sa prisohan. Mao na nga ang education karun, maoy saviour sa ka-gutom ug ka-pobre sa tao.

Out of the 43, those who will graduate from college will only be 21. Out of 100, 21 graduates from college. Where are the 79? Most of them will probably enroll in prison. That is our education today, the saviour from hunger and poverty of the people.

Matud pa ni Bill Gates "I will not blame you if you are born poor, because you cannot do anything about it. But I will blame you if you will die poor because you have done nothing for yourself." In fact, that policy of Kennedy, "Ask not what your government can do to you, but ask what you can do to your government".

Mahimo na natug i-adjust dinhi karon sa Pilipinas. Sa America mahimo na nila kay ang ilang middle income 87%. Ang ilang poverty line, 7% ra. Ang ato diri, bali. Seventy seven% ang below, 15% ray middle income, gawas niadtong 7% nga multi-millionaire.

We can adjust that here in the Philippines. That can be done in the United States since 87% are middle income. Their poverty line is only 7%. Here in the Philippines, it's the other way around. Seventy seven% is below (the poverty line), only 15% is middle income, outside of the 7% who are multi-millionaires.

Pangutana karon sa inyong mga silingan, sa inyong mga lungsod. Ug duna moy kwarta—gawas lag maka daug sa lotto ha, pirti tingali nag daug, kay sobra na—, unsa may inyong gamiton sa kwarta? Number one pagkaun, ika duha, pagpaeskwela sa among mga anak.

Ask the neighbors of your towns. If you have money—unless you win in the lotto (lottery game), a big win, with extra money—what will your money be used for? Number one, food. The second one, for the education of our children.

Unsa man gyuy kaugmaon nato, gawas sa pagpa eskwela? Kung dunay silingan nga mo ingun, "Dili oi. Makadawat mig kwarta, ang primiro namong buhaton, bayad sa utang! Sunod na ng uban." Tungod kay, we are in a quagmire of power. (right hand moving back and forth)

What is really our future, outside of going to school? If you have neighbors who would say, "No, not really. If we receive money, the first thing we will do is pay our debts! The rest will follow." That's because, we are in a quagmire of power.

Statistics that is given by the Philippine Overseas Employment Agency, and the DTI and the NEDA: There is (are) 21 billion dollars, remitted by Filipino overseas to the country. And that is what is making our country good.

Ug wa pa ng kwartaha ambot nalang unsa say mahitabo nato.

If not for that money, I am not sure what will happen to us.

Now who are those people? *Kinsa man ng mga tawhana?* (Who are those people?) *Ang mga college graduates.* (The college graduates.)

Ninety percent of them are the college graduates. TESDA-trained skills workers, engineers, technicians, nurses, doctors, who are the product of our education.

When we had a meeting with all presidents of colleges, pero ako nagtubo kung engineer, daghan kug award sa pagka engineer, pero nahipaluyo na ang akong pagka engineer kay doctor naman ilang itawag nako. Because I took up Doctorate of Education, because of education.

When we had a meeting with all presidents of colleges, but I grew up as an engineer, I have many awards as an engineer but my being an engineer is in the background, since they call me doctor now. Because I took up Doctorate in Education, because of education.

We will go to the education of our people. When we had a meeting with the presidents of all colleges, and CHED announced: "We will go into the training of our colleges, to come up with academic excellence, comparable, with international standards." When it was my turn to talk in the open forum I said, "Yes, we don't have any argument on that. But you please (raising his voice) challenge, channel most our resources to the training of the..."

Reference:
Mr. Doroteo M. Salazar voted as one of the Ten Outstanding Cebuanos. Part 1 of 2. August 20, 2011. (10 minutes)
https://www.youtube.com/watch?v=RAY0wsfw1Tg

Part 2:

... to be awarded, in all awards that I have received from college, coronation as King of Engineers, as Topnotcher, as Outstanding Professional, before, Papal Awardee, but this is the award that I like most, that creeps... (emphasis with a forward-moving hand gesture) (audience clapping loudly) into the life of every Cebuano. And my policy is...

My grandson said, 'Why are you happy papa?'. I am happy because, all of you, my children, and grandchildren are happy. And now, I am happy because what we have, with my wife, made thousands (raising his voice with emphasis) of people happy.

How was this done? How much are you paying for education? Sixteen thousand per semester. How much are we charging our students in Bantayan Island and here in Cebu? All of them (raising his voice) are Cardinal Vidal scholars, paying only four thousand pesos per semester (audience clapping), just to give them the life (audience clapping), to take a profession.

That amounts to something like, forty two million (Philippines pesos) a semester, eighty four million a year, just to give something for our people to be happy. That is an award. And that is what we are doing. And I know all these awardees will be happy having this award. But happier than that is...you can make thousands of people happy.

Thank you and Good Evening. (audience applaud loudly) (Music plays as he steps down the podium, while the Emcee comes up to shake his hand, both with big smiles.)

Reference:
Mr. Doroteo M. Salazar voted as one of the Ten Outstanding Cebuanos. Part 2 of 2. August 20, 2011 (2.10 minutes)
https://www.youtube.com/watch?v=6ZPmuxFk51I

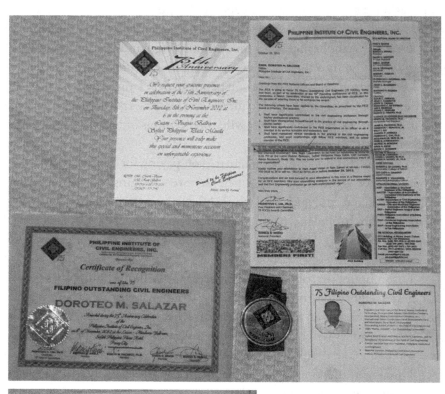

CONGRATULATIONS

DR. DOROTEO M. SALAZAR

Awarded as One of the Most

OUTSTANDING FILIPINO CIVIL

ENGINEERS OF THE CENTURY

November 8, 2012

Sofitel Philippine Plaza, Manila

(Above) Daddy's own collection.

(Left Daddy encoded this sheet, printed it out, and wrote on the bottom, as a label of an envelope storing documents of his achievements.

Appendix 2

Transcript of A Virtual Interview with Mommy

9:25-9:50am, Over brunch, dining Room
September 7, 2021, Guadalupe, Cebu City, Philippines

BV: Why did you and daddy open the school?
ZS: Because many requested
BV: I heard your tuition is low.
ZS: Yes, its lower than other schools.
BV: Are you not losing?
ZS: We get income from our apartment rentals to pay the salaries of the teachers.
BV: I heard you give Cardinal Vidal Scholarships.
ZS: Yes, they pay small tuition, tuition only.
BV: How do the students pay?
ZS: They write promissory notes and pay when they can.
BV: What if they will graduate?
ZS: They cannot get their school records. Then they have to pay little by little.
BV: But how do you pay taxes?
ZS: Pay little by little
AS: By promissory note also! (everyone laughs)
BV: Do you still go to the office?
ZS: Yes!
AS: Or the office comes to us.
BV: Like working from home?
AS: Yes!
BV: Did you use to dance in the plaza across the church?
(ZS lightens up)
ZS: Yes I like to dance.
BV: Did you teach daddy to dance?

ZS: The *bayot* (gay) of Normal (Cebu Normal College) taught him how to dance. Daddy took two weeks of dancing lessons with him.

BV: Did daddy like it?

ZS: If he did not know how to dance, I will dance with anybody during fiesta! So daddy had to learn to dance so that he can dance with me.

BV: Remember you were a public schoolteacher? You taught in Buhisan and Toledo? Why did you stop?

ZS: Nobody will run the office of daddy.

BV: What year was that?

ZS: 1980

BV: What year did you also stop teaching?

ZS: 1980 also

Mommy worked from home during the COVID-19 pandemic. Her loyal office staff brought paperwork to her. Guadalupe, Cebu. April 2022, the year before she passed.

Appendix 3

Transcript of Anthony's 'Eulogy for My Grandfather'

When: July 30, 2017
Where: Our Lady of China Chapel, Sacred Heart Parish, Cebu City, Philippines

Good Evening everyone! "Good Evening!" (audience greets back) To tell you the truth I'm feeling so nervous that I just had to write it down. I typed it too, Please bear with me, this might be a little long for you, but I hope I can keep this under 15 minutes. So please forgive me if I go over 15 minutes (giggles from the audience).

Mayor, School Administrator, and Engineer, a leader, a public servant, a lover, a gentleman, a speaker, a toastmaster, a storyteller gifted by God with wit and humour.

This (centering daddy's picture on the Holy Mass table) was my Papa, my grandfather.

Good Evening! My name is Anthony Gerard. I am 31 years old, representing his 20 grandchildren. As the eldest, Papa called me, Manoy (giggles from the audience). In the Salazar family I am letter 'G'. My wife is a Japanese Christian and I have two kids. Aika Belle 'B' and Daiki Joshua 'D'.

My grandfather wanted to really visit us in Japan this month, to meet his first great grandson. But it was not in God's will. I really wanted to see him before he passed away, but I could not make it back in time. There's deep pain in my heart. But thank you so much for being here to join our family as we grieve, although we are glad to be reunited now, as a family. It will take time for our hearts to heal.

My heart goes out to my grandmother. Mama, we love you. After we all return to different countries: Japan, the States, Canada, Australia, please pray for deep comfort and peace, that can only come through Jesus Christ.

These are four things that I remember about Papa:

1. A Role-model
   Papa was not born wealthy. Against all odds, through hard work and perseverance, he managed to build a legacy of public service. God gave Papa a desire to help the underprivileged. Papa provided scholarships through his college, Salazar Institute of Technology. Papa was a man for the masses, because he himself experienced hardship and poverty.

2. Papa was a provider.
   My Uncle Adam told me that we, grandkids, are a privileged generation. I heard that Papa changed when he became a grandfather. I heard he was extremely strict to my mom and her siblings. But later in his life he became a whole lot more lenient.

   I hardly recall a moment when Papa refused our demands. I think we were spoiled. You're nodding your head. But with all seriousness, Papa (pointing to the picture on the Holy Mass table), looked out for all of us, and made sure that all over needs were met.

Before I left for Japan in 2010, to pursue a career in Japan, I tried hard to sell my video camcorder, to save up money. Where's my mom? Is my mom sitting here somewhere? Oh, hi! (Waving at me at the back of the seated crowd, while I waved back to him) my mom remembers this! In vain, I tried to sell my video camcorder but I could not find a willing buyer. Finally, my mom found someone! Guess who? (audience giggles loudly) Papa (pointing to daddy's picture on the Holy Mass table). He bought it from me so that he could use it for the school, to help me and the school.

Another time in a visit here in 2015, papa approached me asked me if I needed financial help. I told him I did not need it but it was still a very moving gesture.

Papa cared. He did. He wanted to support me. And thanks to him, I now work as a Pastoral Intern in a Christian Missionary team, and also as an English teacher in Japan.

3. Papa was a kind passionate supporter.
    Let me tell you three stories.

I spoke to Lola Flor, she's in here. (Audience murmurs and giggles while Emily focused the cell phone camera towards Auntie Flor, who gave a big smile, waved both of her arms and bowed to the audience. Emily said 'Mama Flor, Mama Flor, she's Mama Flor', hoping Anthony could hear it).

I'm sorry Mama Flor. She's my grandfather's sister and I spoke to her yesterday.

They were 10 siblings. My grandfather was number 4? (nodding his head with the audience). I've heard that Papa continued to support his siblings, and my grandmother's siblings, while taking care of his own family.

I talked to our family driver, Roy, a couple of years ago. Roy told me that he's indebted to Papa for all the times he asked for extra money- for his family. Roy was not a family member but Papa was a man of compassion and mercy.

And I also heard in the past 30 years that Papa made it a point to provide a college education for our household maids and their children. I've heard comments growing up, from the maids and family drivers, that Papa was a kind boss.

4. Papa was a father figure.
Although Papa was extremely busy all the time, he would always try to give each of us his attention, and show interest. He would affectionately greet us grandkids with his "I will hear the head!", where he pretended to read our minds and tell us what we were thinking.

I remember the days when we would take naps in his room, in the afternoons, and then he would treat us to pizza, fast food, or ice cream.

He called us grandkids - and my Uncle Eduardo told me, not many people know this. He called us grandkids, God's Good Children, for GOCHI. Why's it GOCHI? Because Good, 'G-O', Children, 'C-H-I', GOCHI, for short. It sounds like a Japanese word.

Until now I did not really care to think about why papa would choose to give credit to God. Maybe

1. Because he knew that each one of us, is from God.
2. Maybe he thought about how each grandchild reminded him of God's goodness, or
3. Maybe he wanted each of us to live for God.

I'd like to conclude with my closing remarks. Brokenness, sadness, regrets, and hope.
We live in a broken world. Lola, F.. I'm sorry. (The voice of Emily, Anthony's younger sister, and the one taking a video of Anthony, could be

heard in the video. She softly said, 'Mama Flor'). (The audience politely giggled.)

I'm sorry. Please forgive me. Mama Flor (as Anthony points a palm toward Auntie Flor) told me this yesterday. And she was very honest. And I think it's good for everyone to hear this. I hope this is ok to share (Looking at Auntie Flor). She's nodding her head, she knows.

She told me this, "It does not make any sense that God would take away a good man, like Papa, while many bad people continue to live."

Where is justice? Is God unfair?

We know that since Adam and Eve rebelled against God as King, we suffered the curse that our sins deserve. Our relationships are broken, our hearts crave security in many god-substitutes, we live for selfish reasons, and pay lip-service to God, and sadly for physical, eternal death is the search and death sentence that we deserve. There's no excuse in the hands of God who is holy.

1. Sadness, sadness

It is ok to cry? Is it ok to weep? Is it even ok to show our true motions? Yes.

In the Gospel according to John Chapter 11, even Jesus wept when he heard that his friend Lazarus had died. Jesus showed his true emotions. Jesus was sad and we can be sad too. Honestly pouring out or hearts and talking to God directly, through Jesus, is the path to healing.

Also, God has given us each other.

2. Regrets, regrets

I regret not making time to call from overseas. I regret not making it back in time for his last breath. I regret not talking to Papa straight about his religious beliefs while he was still strong. I was afraid of offending my grandfather but underneath my fear was my lack of love for him.

You see, if you really love someone you would tell him the truth. Love and truth go together, even if its an inconvenient truth.

And I'm sure we all have regrets. But God offers us complete forgiveness now. And God works out all our mistakes for His Glory, for our good, and to move on with courage.

So lastly, Hope.

When I think about Papa's qualities: role model, provider, supporter, father figure, I cannot help but reflect on how he reflected the image of God in his life.

Jesus is our Hope, the ultimate servant, leader, role model. God is our ultimate provider, supporter, and Heavenly Father.

It's ok to share my mom, my mother had a private moment with my Papa at his bedside. My mother told me that Papa nodded, "Yes!", to receive Jesus as his personal Lord and Saviour. My last words to Papa on midnight, at midnight, was long distance call last week. Wednesday. My mom, my Aunt Cecile, and my Uncle Eduardo were in the room.

I regret not seeing Papa face-to-face. And I basically said this, I said that "Faith is trust." And I encouraged him to trust God because there is complete healing, complete healing in heaven. I told him that only Jesus died with the full penalty of sin. And only Jesus can take him to paradise because Jesus never breaks His promise.

Dear Friends help me recall the words. On the cross Jesus said, "Why have you forsaken me?" (with the audience saying "forsaken me" in chorus). Thank you. Why have you forsaken me? Jesus was forsaken, so that we could be forgiven.

And Jesus said on the cross, "It is finished." (with the audience saying "done", "finished", in chorus). And we can rest spiritually, only because of the finished work of Jesus.

Jesus, the one and only mediator, is the only way Papa and I can see each other again. And Jesus is the only way and the only hope for you too.

Here's one last question before I close.

Many of us hoped for mercy. We prayed hard, but did God ignore our prayers for Papa's healing now that he passed away?

This I know. Whether God heals miraculously now, or gets complete healing later in heaven, God always does what is right. And Heaven is not wishful thinking. We were created for him. God has placed eternity in our hearts. Heaven is where our true citizenship is. And we talked about the resurrection, just a Jesus had a bodily, physical, resurrection, our future hope is the same.

And if you don't mind me being funny, that means, there will be a real physical, reunion with pizza, fast food, ice cream, and karaoke, that will never end (some in the audience were nodding). No more crying, no more sadness.

And as Job in the bible said, "The Lord gives and the Lord takes away." But Blessed be His name! Let us be thankful for God. I'm sorry. Let us be thankful to God, for Papa's life.

To God be the Glory, and our memories of Papa, will stay in our hearts, and nothing will take that away.

One last thing before I close. Did I speak under 15 minutes? (audience giggling). If you don't mind, I'm going to sing a song, If it's ok.

I was talking to Tita Ellen at the back. And I was looking at the list (referring to the list of songs sang by the invited group of singers).

I was so surprised because when Papa went to my wedding in Japan in 2011, I chose three Christian songs: I chose, "As the Deer", which is my wife's favorite song. Number 2, I chose, "Great is thy Faithfulness". And it's perfect timing that this next song is the song that I'm about to sing. It's probably a song that you never heard. But It's a song that Papa got to sing in my wedding. And I hope that you would listen to me and think deeply about its words.

This song is called, "In Christ Alone". You know this song? (audience nods and some say, "Yes") Oh! Wow!

References:
https://youtu.be/pNCs9YQWT6g?si=Z-IAWiLVOUiQYFc3
Scan this QR code to listen to the eulogy.

About the Author

Dr. Beth Salazar Villarin is the second child and eldest daughter of Engr. Doroteo Monte de ramos Salazar and Mrs. Zenaida Figuracion Salazar. She finished her preparatory, elementary, and high school years at St. Theresa's College, Cebu City, Philippines.

She graduated *Magna Cum Laude* at the University of San Carlos, Cebu City, Philippines, with the degree of Bachelor of Science in Business Administration, Major in Economics. Three years later she completed her Master of Business Administration at the National University, San Diego, California. Fifteen years later, she graduated Doctor of Philosophy in Education at the University of San Carlos.

In May 2019, she completed her Diploma in Early Childhood Education at Algonquin College, Ottawa, Ontario, Canada, with honors. She had undergone other certificate programs and trainings in the Philippines, United States, and Canada in the fields of real estate, sales, computer programming, medical office administration, among others.

Dr. Villarin currently sits in the Board of Salazar Colleges of Science and Institute of Technology (SCSIT), Cebu, Philippines. She divides her time travelling between the various school campuses in the Philippines and occasionally visiting her six children and six grandchildren abroad.

She would be glad to hear from you. You may chat with her at: chatwithbethsv@gmail.com Check her website for interesting insights. shareawordwithme.wordpress.com

Beth listened intently to Marlinda Angbetic-Tan, her Editor.

Marlinda is a thespian, a distinguished English and Cebuano writer, and a founding officer and past chairperson of WILA, Women in Literary Arts, Inc. (2001-2003), the only women creative writers' group in the Philippines. She became the Executive Editor of the Lifestyle section and the monthly magazine of "The Freeman", Cebu's oldest newspaper (2002-2012). She was the Central Visayas coordinator in the sub-committee on Literary Arts of the NCCA, National Commission on Culture & Arts directly under the Office of the President of the Philippines (2001-2007).

Cebu City, Philippines. April 30, 2023.

Printed in the United States
by Baker & Taylor Publisher Services